On

Congratulations! You r. the Principles of Economics concepts that you will learn in this book. These downloadable templates will help you implement your learnings in the real world and give you an in-depth understanding of the concepts.

The templates include solved practice exercises based on each chapter. The solved questions will help you test your knowledge and enhance your academic preparation. The question types include:

- Mathematical problems
- Scenario-based questions
- Discussion questions

To access the templates, follow the steps below:

- Go to www.vibrantpublishers.com
- Click on the 'Online Resources' option on the Home Page
- Login by entering your account details (or create an account if you don't have one)
- Go to the Self-Learning Management series section on the Online Resources page
- Click the 'Principles of Economics Essentials You Always Wanted To Know' link and access the templates.

Happy self-learning!

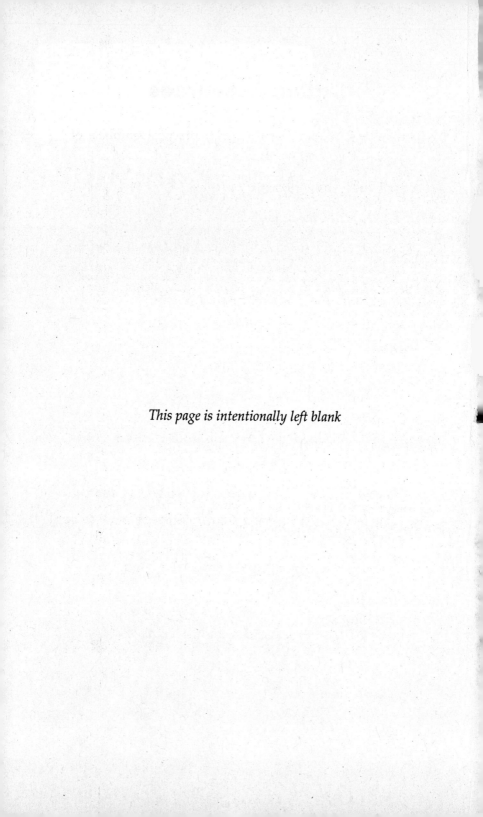

This page is intentionally left blank

VIBRANT
PUBLISHERS

PRINCIPLES OF ECONOMICS ESSENTIALS

YOU ALWAYS WANTED TO KNOW

Economics simplified like never before

CLEDWYN FERNANDEZ

Principles of Economics Essentials You Always Wanted To Know

Paperback ISBN 10: 1-63651-233-X
Paperback ISBN 13: 978-1-63651-233-4

Ebook ISBN 10: 1-63651-234-8
Ebook ISBN 13: 978-1-63651-234-1

Hardback ISBN 10: 1636512356
Hardback ISBN 13: 978-1-63651-235-8

Library of Congress Control Number: 2024937276

Vibrant Publishers books are available at special quantity discount for sales promotions, or for use in corporate training programs. For more information please write to bulkorders@vibrantpublishers.com

Please email feedback / corrections (technical, grammatical or spelling) to spellerrors@vibrantpublishers.com

To access the complete catalogue of Vibrant Publishers, visit www.vibrantpublishers.com

SELF-LEARNING MANAGEMENT SERIES

TITLE	PAPERBACK* ISBN
ACCOUNTING, FINANCE & ECONOMICS	
COST ACCOUNTING AND MANAGEMENT ESSENTIALS	9781636511030
FINANCIAL ACCOUNTING ESSENTIALS	9781636510972
FINANCIAL MANAGEMENT ESSENTIALS	9781636511009
MACROECONOMICS ESSENTIALS	9781636511818
MICROECONOMICS ESSENTIALS	9781636511153
PERSONAL FINANCE ESSENTIALS	9781636511849
PRINCIPLES OF ECONOMICS ESSENTIALS	9781636512334
ENTREPRENEURSHIP & STRATEGY	
BUSINESS COMMUNICATION ESSENTIALS	9781636511634
BUSINESS PLAN ESSENTIALS	9781636511214
BUSINESS STRATEGY ESSENTIALS	9781949395778
ENTREPRENEURSHIP ESSENTIALS	9781636511603
GENERAL MANAGEMENT	
BUSINESS LAW ESSENTIALS	9781636511702
DATA ANALYTICS ESSENTIALS	9781636511184
DECISION MAKING ESSENTIALS	9781636510026
LEADERSHIP ESSENTIALS	9781636510316
PRINCIPLES OF MANAGEMENT ESSENTIALS	9781636511542
TIME MANAGEMENT ESSENTIALS	9781636511665

*Also available in Hardback & Ebook formats

SELF-LEARNING MANAGEMENT SERIES

TITLE	PAPERBACK* ISBN

HUMAN RESOURCE MANAGEMENT

DIVERSITY IN THE WORKPLACE ESSENTIALS	9781636511122
HR ANALYTICS ESSENTIALS	9781636510347
HUMAN RESOURCE MANAGEMENT ESSENTIALS	9781949395839
ORGANIZATIONAL BEHAVIOR ESSENTIALS	9781636510378
ORGANIZATIONAL DEVELOPMENT ESSENTIALS	9781636511481

MARKETING & SALES MANAGEMENT

DIGITAL MARKETING ESSENTIALS	9781949395747
MARKETING MANAGEMENT ESSENTIALS	9781636511788
SALES MANAGEMENT ESSENTIALS	9781636510743
SERVICES MARKETING ESSENTIALS	9781636511733
SOCIAL MEDIA MARKETING ESSENTIALS	9781636512181

OPERATIONS & PROJECT MANAGEMENT

AGILE ESSENTIALS	9781636510057
OPERATIONS & SUPPLY CHAIN MANAGEMENT ESSENTIALS	9781949395242
PROJECT MANAGEMENT ESSENTIALS	9781636510712
STAKEHOLDER ENGAGEMENT ESSENTIALS	9781636511511

*Also available in Hardback & Ebook formats

About the Author

 **Cledwyn Fernandez** is an economist and has worked in academia and policy organizations. His current profile is a Fellow at The Indian Council for Research on International Economic Relations. As a Fellow at ICRIER, he works with government ministries, private sector enterprises, multilateral development banks, and multilateral organizations for a wide range of economic projects including labor markets, gender and development, energy, and the digital economy. Cledwyn holds a Ph.D. in Economics from XLRI, Jamshedpur, India, and is a gold medallist in M.A., Economics from Christ University, Bangalore, India. Post his Ph.D., Cledwyn started his career as an Assistant Professor of Economics at T.A. Pai Management Institute (TAPMI), Manipal, India, where he taught subjects including Microeconomics, Macroeconomics, and Economic Policy and Analysis. His research interests lie in areas of development economics, impact evaluation, and public policy. Cledwyn has published research papers in the areas of international trade and financial inclusion in international journals. He has also published case studies in leading case journals including Harvard Publishing/Ivey, Case Centre, and Emerald Emerging Market Case Studies.

What experts say about this book!

This book consists of 12 chapters highlighting three important aspects of economics, that is, the consumer, the producer, and the market. It illustrates all the basics of micro and macroeconomic theories that provide a way for economists to analyze and predict the behavior of financial markets and the economy.

The chapters inside this book highlight the above information with examples, which will help the readers understand the concepts in a better way. The way this book is written encourages the reader to finish it at a stretch. Many examples and relations are drawn not just from mathematics or statistics but also from aesthetic literature. This book goes beyond the conventional understanding of the meaning of economics and does an excellent job of it.

– Dr. Raj Seshadri, Professor,
Jawaharlal Business School, Palakkad

The book is well laid out and easy to follow. The content is informed and up to date. It is easy to use and well-designed.

– Jack Wiley, Academic Dean of Instruction,
Trinidad State College, Alamosa Colorado

Table of Contents

Preface

Economics is a subject that applies to all aspects of life. Simplistically put, economics is the study of choices, decisions, and resource allocations in an economy. How do consumers decide how to spend their money? How do producers decide which product to sell, or at what price? Why do monopolies exist? How do firms compete with one another? Why do governments provide basic infrastructure services at subsidized costs? How does an economy work? The answer to all these questions lies in this book.

Economics is often dreaded as a subject that is complicated and difficult to comprehend. This book, *Principles of Economics,* tries to debunk that thought by making economics simple and yet fun to learn. This is a book for everyone. You may be a school student aiming to pursue economics as a college degree, a young working professional looking to learn some basic economics for your work, or even someone far away from the world of economics, but wanting to understand how this subject is related to life. This book has been written keeping in mind the broader audience who will probably be entering the world of economics for the first time. Each chapter in this book contains real-life applications that complement the theoretical concepts. These examples will enable the reader to relate to the economic concepts much better.

After reading this book, readers will be able to understand the functioning of an economy. The goal of this book is to equip readers with the tools to analyze real-life events with an economic lens. This will provide the readers with a better understanding of economic events and will improve how they can integrate the learnings of economics into day-to-day decision-making. For instance, if you are a seller producing a product or service in the market, this book will help you understand the functioning of a market economy better, providing you with the tools for improving production in a cost-effective way. As a consumer, you will become aware of the reasons behind price increases or decreases, how consumer preferences work, and the principles of elasticity.

While reading each chapter of this book, it is advised that the readers apply the concepts in each chapter to the real-life examples surrounding them. The content in this book can be leveraged only by applying these principles in the things you do or see in real life.

I hope you enjoy reading this book and embrace economics in a much better way than you did before you started reading this book. Most of the examples in this book are contextualized for the United States. However, readers and instructors can find similar examples that apply to them.

How to use this book?

This book consists of three sections and 12 Chapters.

1. Section 1 of the book deals with consumer theory. This section consists of four chapters, with topics such as the market economy, understanding demand and supply, and consumer behavior. It starts by discussing the ten basic principles of economics and then continues by integrating the role of demand and supply in an economy (Chapters 1 and 2). Chapter 3 lays out the concepts of elasticity, while Chapter 4 discusses consumer behavior and its applications in the determination of price, preferences, and product choices.

2. Section 2 of the book deals with producer theory. This section consists of two chapters. Chapter 5 starts with a discussion of the theory of production. It covers the concepts of factors of production, productivity, and all the theories related to a firm's production. Chapter 6 initiates the discussion on the cost of production. It discusses the different types of cost structures that a firm faces and provides a deeper understanding of how producers can achieve cost-effective ways of production.

3. Section 3 of the book deals with market structures. This section consists of three chapters. Chapter 7 analyzes the first type of market structure, called perfect competition. Chapter 8 then introduces the opposite of perfect competition, namely, monopoly. Chapter 9 discusses the most common type of market structure, called oligopoly. This chapter also discusses the application of game theory in market structures. Overall, this section touches upon how

firms set prices, how output is determined, and the level of interaction with other firms in an economy.

4. The last and final section of this book is an introduction to Macroeconomics. It consists of three chapters. Chapter 10 focuses on the computation of the national income of an economy and introduces the key concepts of national income accounting. Chapter 11 continues this discussion by delving into the components of aggregate demand and the role of the government in stimulating the economy. Lastly, Chapter 12 concludes by touching upon two important economic policies–the fiscal policy undertaken by the government, and the monetary policy implemented by the central bank of the country.

This book has been written with the purpose of making the reader understand the building blocks of an economy (Microeconomics), and then putting the pieces together to understand the functioning of the larger economy (Macroeconomics). The first part of the book contains 9 chapters that deal with microeconomic concepts, while the second part of the book contains 3 chapters that deal with macroeconomic concepts. It is advised that the readers read the book in the same order to get the narrative in place. The chapter summary at the end discusses the key points that are to be kept in mind. Each chapter also has a few multiple-choice questions (MCQs) which test the learnings from the chapter.

Who can benefit from this book?

The short answer is–everyone! This book has key takeaway messages for every reader, depending on your role in society. If you are a consumer who purchases goods and services from the market, Chapters 1-4 are for you. If you are a producer that sells your goods or services in a market, Chapters 5-9 are for you. Lastly, if you are someone in a governmental role or with a policy background, Chapters 10–12, which focus on national income and overall macroeconomics, may be of interest to you. While certain chapters of the book may appeal more to certain sections of readers, the book in its entirety is a story. Reading parts of the book may not give you the complete picture of the economy. This book can also be used as teaching material for an introductory course in Economics. It is advised that all readers read the complete book, and apply the necessary learnings in their daily life or business.

This page is intentionally left blank

Chapter 1

An Introduction to the World of Economics

E conomics is the study of human behavior. Economics deals with the interaction among stakeholders in the economy, including consumers (individuals), producers (firms), and the government. Economics is broadly categorized into microeconomics and macroeconomics. Microeconomics deals with the study of individuals and firms. Macroeconomics deals with the study of nations.

This chapter will deal with the central themes in economics. It will discuss the ten key guiding principles of economics. The key questions that are discussed using the central themes are the following: How do individuals allocate resources? How do firms allocate resources to maximize profits and welfare? How do governments allocate resources to maximize well-being? Resources are finite and scarce. Therefore, a robust mechanism must exist by which resources are efficiently allocated across all stakeholders in an economy.

The key learning objectives of this chapter include the reader's understanding of the following:

- The ten guiding principles of economic decision-making

- The different principles concerning households, firms, and the government

- Applying these principles in further applications of economic concepts

1.1 The Ten Principles of Economics

Economics, as a discipline, is guided by ten broad principles.[1] These principles are the building blocks that aid consumers and producers in their decision-making. Each of these principles has multiple applications in real-life decision-making. These ten principles are divided into three categories: how people make decisions, how people interact, and how the economy as a whole works.

1.1.1 How people make decisions

a. Individuals face trade-offs

Decision-making involves choosing among choices. As a consumer, one must decide whether to invest their savings in interest-bearing assets or purchasing a car. Similarly, imagine

---

1. Mankiw, N.G (2018) Principles of Economics, Cengage

a producer selling their products across multiple states in the country. The producer must decide whether to focus on localization first (thereby gaining market share in a particular location) or to expand to other states quickly (gain market share across the country). These choices are associated with a trade-off. Given that resources are limited while choosing one, you give up the other. Trade-offs are central to decision-making. This is because resources are finite and individuals must allocate their resources in a manner that will maximize their objectives. Governments also face a trade-off between efficiency and equity. When the government decides to allocate financial resources across sectors in an economy, the most important trade-off that it makes is between equity (equal access) and efficiency (complete utilization).

b. The cost of something is what you give up to get it

Given that trade-offs are central to decision-making by both firms and households, a trade-off comes with an associated cost. This cost is termed an opportunity cost. An opportunity cost of some item is the cost of something that we give up to get that item. Imagine that you are planning to attend graduate school and enroll yourself in a two-year program. You are currently working in a job that is paying you a certain amount. The opportunity cost of attending graduate school is not only the monetary cost of the education (fees) but also the associated loss in income over the next two years that you will forgo. Thus, opportunity cost is also termed as an implicit cost. It is important to mention here that the opportunity cost is not always monetary and also includes time and other intangible resources associated with the decision.

c. People think at the margin

Thinking at the margin is an essential principle of economics. Thinking at the margin essentially implies making decisions while keeping in mind the additional input or output. For example, assume you are a producer of shoes and own a shoe manufacturing company. You decide to hire an extra worker. However, you are unsure of the value addition to the total output of shoes by employing the additional worker. In this context, the marginal cost is the additional cost incurred in hiring the worker. If the marginal benefit is higher than the marginal cost, it will make economic sense to hire the worker. This kind of rational thinking is called thinking at the margin.

d. People respond to incentives

Incentives drive human behavior, and markets respond to incentives. Business decisions are a function of incentives that are provided by the government. Similarly, consumer demand is a function of the incentives provided by producers. In scenarios when the government lowers the corporate tax rate, businesses respond by producing more and are incentivized to conduct more business because of the lower tax regime. Similarly, when producers provide sale offers during a certain period of time, it leads to higher demand. Hence, individuals and firms respond to incentives which get reflected in the market through prices.

Apart from producers and consumers, it is important that government and policymakers understand how incentives work, and how individuals react to incentives. For instance, a lower tax on electric vehicles would have a positive impact on the adoption of electric vehicles by consumers, thereby positively impacting the climate. Similarly, by providing subsidies to manufacturers, the production of electric vehicles will increase. Therefore, understanding how a particular incentive works for a particular section of stakeholders in an economy is crucial.

1.1.2 How people interact

a. Trade can make everyone better off

Trade is the exchange of goods and services across different entities. The parties in a transaction can be individuals or countries. But what is the basis on which trade takes place? There are two key economic concepts that are the basis for economic trade. The first is called **absolute advantage**, and the second is called **comparative advantage**. Absolute advantage is defined as the ability to produce goods using fewer inputs than another producer.[2] Let us take an example of the coffee market in the United States. Imagine that Starbucks could provide the same quality of coffee as compared to its competitors at a much lower price due to a unique cost advantage that it gains through its technology. If this happens, Starbucks will have an absolute advantage in producing coffee over all its competitors. Comparative advantage, on the other hand, is defined as the ability to produce goods at a lower opportunity cost than another producer.[3]

Remember, the word opportunity cost is crucial here. What does it mean? Take the same example where there are two coffee retail outlets, namely, Starbucks and Costa Coffee. Each of them produces two goods: Cinnamon buns and coffee. However, Starbucks can produce coffee at $2 per cup, and a

2. Mankiw, N.G (2018) Principles of Economics, Cengage

3. ibid

cinnamon bun at $5 per bun. On the other hand, Costa Coffee can produce coffee at $2.50 per cup and a cinnamon bun at $3 per bun. Hence, Starbucks should trade coffee in exchange for cinnamon buns. What is important to understand is how countries or firms accrue these advantages. One important mechanism that allows firms to gain these advantages is the productivity levels of workers and access to technological infrastructure. Greater use of technology and increased productivity are two important sources of absolute and comparative advantage.

b. Markets are a good way to organize economic activity

A market is defined as a group of buyers and sellers. While sellers decide what to produce and how much to produce, consumers decide how much to buy. But what decides the allocation and quantity of the goods that are being exchanged? The deciding factor is the price. The product is sold when the buyers and sellers reach a price level that is acceptable to both. While markets were mostly physical, today the market economy consists of the digital sphere too, such as the e-commerce organizations and the platform economy which brings the buyers and sellers onto a platform.

Adam Smith, a philosopher of the 18th century, was the first person to study the functioning of markets. His book, *The Wealth of Nations* published in the year 1776 talks about how markets work. His concept of the **invisible hand** is central to the functioning of a marketplace. The premise of the invisible hand is that government intervention is kept to the minimum and the market forces drive the demand and supply of goods.

c. Governments can improve market outcomes

The government plays a crucial role in the development of an
economy. Why does the government intervene in the market,
if the market organizes economic activity efficiently? One
reason for government intervention is the misallocation of
resources that leads to **market failure**. A market failure exists
when the production or consumption of goods and services by
the market is not efficient. There are multiple reasons for such
a market failure to occur. One important factor leading to a
market failure is known as an **externality**.

Externalities are indirect effects of consumption or production
activities. Externalities can be positive as well as negative.
A good example of a positive externality was seen during
COVID. The appropriate use of masks and ensuring complete
vaccination was helpful not only to oneself but also to the
people around.

On the other hand, if a firm that is manufacturing steel pollutes
the nearby river causing difficulty for other individuals
and firms to co-exist, it leads to a negative externality. The
government plays a critical role by intervening in the market
and correcting any form of negative externality. Through taxes
and subsidies, the government tries to correct market failure
and ensure that the allocation of resources is optimal.

1.1.3 How the economy as a whole works

a. A country's standard of living depends on its ability to produce things that other people want to buy

Why are some countries rich while others are poor? The
differences in income per capita across economies are visible
in the quality of life.[4] What explains this difference? One

---

4. Income per capita is defined as the income divided by the number of people in the
economy

reason is that richer economies have workers who are more productive and can produce more goods for fewer hours or work, thereby gaining a better advantage. This advantage leads to higher income levels that improve the standard of living for individuals. Governments across the world continue to provide ways to improve living standards for their people. While providing subsidies to the poor is a temporary solution, mechanisms such as improved education and better access to food, and health facilities are more long-term solutions that can help improve the output of an economy, and thereby lead to a higher standard of living.

b. Prices rise when the government prints too much money

Inflation is defined as the increase in prices of goods and services in an economy. The Central Banks of economies are responsible for keeping inflation in check. Through their policies, they can either increase or reduce interest rates which regulate money supply in the economy. An increase in the supply of money leads to higher inflation, while a reduction in the supply of money lowers inflation. [5] The monetary policy, which is the key policy of the bank, is the tool by which inflation rates are kept in check. Through its policies, the central bank can either increase or reduce the supply of money in an economy. An increase in the supply of money leads to higher inflation, while a reduction in the supply of money lowers inflation. The monetary policy, which is the key policy of the bank, is the tool by which inflation rates are kept in check.

---

5. The central bank changes the money supply by altering the interest rates. This shall be discussed in further chapters in the book.

c. Society faces a short-run trade-off between inflation and unemployment.

Inflation and unemployment are two evils that the government is always on a mission to reduce. However, in the short run, there is always a trade-off between the two. In other words, if inflation is kept under check, then unemployment remains large, while when unemployment is low, inflation kicks off. In essence, lower prices in the economy are the result of high unemployment, while higher prices are the result of low unemployment. The relationship between inflation and unemployment is termed the Phillips Curve. [6] The reasoning for this inverse relationship is that when the money supply in an economy increases (people have more cash to spend), the purchasing power for goods and services increases. This increases the incentive for producers to produce more. To match the increased cost of production, the price of goods and services starts to rise. Hence, an inverse relationship exists between inflation and unemployment in an economy. This relationship however holds true mostly in the short run. In the long run, as individuals adapt their expectations about future inflationary pressures, the relationship does not hold true.

1.2 Conclusion

These ten principles form the core of economics. It would be beneficial to keep these ten principles in mind while reading through the book, as the application of these principles will come to light in various chapters going forward. These principles are the building blocks of various economic theories.

---

6. William Phillips, a New Zealand born economist, wrote a paper in 1958 titled "The Relation between Unemployment and the Rate of Change of Money Wage Rates in the United Kingdom, 1861–1957", which was published in the quarterly journal Economica.

Quiz

1. **Allocation of resources is important in an economy because resources are _____.**

   a. scarce

   b. abundant

   c. costly

   d. shared

2. **What are the different types of externalities?**

   a. Positive externality

   b. Negative externality

   c. Neutral externality

   d. Both a and b

3. **The relationship between inflation and unemployment in an economy is:**

   a. Positive

   b. Inverse

   c. Cannot be determined

   d. Inverse only in the short run

4. **The opportunity cost of going for a higher education is**

   _____.

   a. The cost associated with the higher education

   b. The cost of the income forgone to opt for higher education

   c. The cost of the future income you will gain

   d. Both a and b

5. **Inflation increases when the government _____ the supply of money.**

   a. increases

   b. decreases

   c. maintains

   d. both a and b

6. **The Phillips curve examines the relationship between _____ and _____.**

   a. Unemployment; output

   b. Inflation; output

   c. Inflation; unemployment

   d. None of the above

7. When factories invest in pollution abatement technologies, it is an example of a _____ externality.

   a. Positive

   b. Negative

   c. Consumption

   d. None of the above

8. Productivity is defined as producing a _____ quantity at a _____ amount of time.

   a. Lower; higher

   b. Higher; lesser

   c. Lower; lesser

   d. Higher, higher

9. _____ advantage is when a country has a lower opportunity cost in the production of a good.

   a. Comparative

   b. Absolute

   c. Exceptional

   d. Both a and b

10. Trade-offs occur in decision-making due to resources being
    _____ .

   a. Limited

   b. Scarce

   c. Abundant

   d. Both a and b

Answers	1 – a	2 – d	3 – d	4 – d	5 – a
	6 – c	7 – a	8 – b	9 – a	10 – d

Chapter Summary

◆ Individuals face trade-offs while making decisions. Decision-making is always done at the margin, and each decision comes with an opportunity cost.

◆ Stakeholders in an economy interact with one another through trade, which has the possibility of making everyone better off. The market economy works best when market forces determine output and prices. Furthermore, the government can improve the market outcome by mitigating market failures through its policies.

◆ Increasing productivity is essential in improving the standard of living of people in an economy. An increase in the supply of money increases inflation, and there is a short-run trade-off between inflation and unemployment.

Chapter 2

Demand, Supply, and the Market Equilibrium

This chapter will build the beginning blocks of the market structure in an economy. It will introduce the concepts of demand and supply and the interactive forces that affect the demand and supply conditions. It will provide the mechanism by which the equilibrium price is decided in the market. Lastly, the chapter will further discuss how government regulations can affect market forces..

The key learning objectives of this chapter include the reader's understanding of the following:

- The driving forces behind the demand and supply conditions in a market

- How economic situations lead to a change in demand and supply

- Evaluating the market equilibrium using demand and supply forces

- Evaluating the effect of government regulations on market forces

2.1 What is a Market?

A market is a place where buyers (consumers), and suppliers (producers) meet together to engage in a meaningful transaction of goods and services. While markets have been traditionally defined as a *physical* space wherein both, the buyers and the sellers meet, the definition today is no longer restricted to only a *physical* medium. In today's digital world, a market can exist on a digital platform where goods and services are exchanged between buyers and sellers. This kind of market is known as the **platform economy**. The platform economy is an economy that is digital in nature and brings together the buyer and seller on a virtual platform. Examples of platform economies are Amazon, Uber, and DoorDash.

2.2 How Markets Determine How Much to Produce, and at What Price to Produce Goods

One of the biggest challenges that a market faces is **price determination**. How do markets decide the quantity and price of an economic good?[7] While the quantity of a good is a function of the size of the market, the price is a function of many other interactive variables. The functioning of a market is dependent on two important variables, namely, demand and supply. A demand-supply framework is a vital framework in microeconomics that is used to study markets of different kinds. For example, have you ever wondered the following: Why do football match tickets become very expensive when a top key player is playing? Why are oil prices so important across the world? How does a good season of rainfall affect the prices of agricultural products? Why do Ivy League universities charge a premium for their education? The answer to all of these lies in understanding the core demand and supply mechanics. All markets can be broken into demand-side components and supply-side components. .

2.2.1 Demand curve

The demand curve is defined as the relationship between the price of the good and the quantity demanded, *ceteris paribus*.[8] Figure 2.1 illustrates the shape of the demand curve. Price is marked on the vertical axis, whereas quantity is marked on the horizontal axis. The downward-sloping line represents a negative relationship between price and quantity demanded. In other words, as price falls from p_1 to p_2 the quantity demanded increases from q_1 to q_2.

Let the quantity demanded for eggs for $10 per egg be one egg. When the price falls to $8, the quantity demanded increases to two eggs. Therefore, the quantity demanded increases from one unit (q_1) to two units (q_2), as the price reduces from $10 ($p_1$) to $8 ($p_2$).

---

7. An economic good is defined as a product or service which can command a price when sold. The term economic good is here onwards used as "good".

8. Ceteris paribus is a Latin phrase which means keeping other things constant

Figure 2.1   **The demand curve**

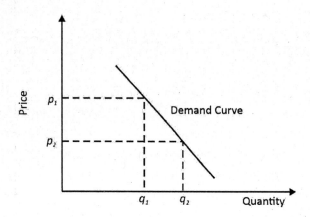

In addition to the price, the demand for goods is dependent on the following factors:

a. **Income:** Income is positively associated with the market demand for goods. If the income of households in an economy increases, it is expected that the demand for goods and services will increase. This will shift the demand curve to the right (see Figure 2.1). On the other hand, if the income of the household declines, then the demand curve will shift to the left. In this regard, it is important to differentiate between two types of goods, namely, **normal goods** and *inferior goods*. For normal goods, higher income leads to higher demand. For inferior goods, higher income leads to lower demand.

Table 2.1 lists out the effect of a change in income on demand for both types of goods. As an example, if margarine is considered to be a lower quality version of butter, then as the income of an individual increases, the demand for margarine will decrease, and that of butter will increase.

Table 2.1	Relationship between income and demand for different types of goods

Type of Goods	Income	Demand
Normal	Increases	Increases
Inferior	Increases	Decreases

b. **Taste and preferences:** Taste and preferences have a significant impact on the demand for goods. It is important to note that while taste and preferences are individualistic, they can also be community-based. Hence, from an organizational point of view, firms must be able to estimate the tastes and preferences of individuals in a certain region before launching products, as it can have a significant effect (positive/negative) on the demand for goods. An example of this is the entry of Starbucks in Australia. Starbucks is a popular coffee chain in the United States. However, on entering the Australian market, it did not succeed well. Despite Australia having a strong and thriving coffee culture, Starbucks failed to adapt to the tastes and preferences of the Australians, forcing them to shut down stores due to rising losses. Starbucks was unable to change the taste of its coffee to match the local coffee preference. Starbucks was unable to change the taste of its coffee to match the local coffee preference.

c. **Market size:** The market size is defined as the total number of consumers in the market. The market size is an important determinant of the demand for goods. If the market size is small, the demand for goods will be small, thereby leading to lower revenues and profitability for the firm. On the contrary, if the market size is large, then the demand for goods will be large. However, it is noteworthy to mention that a larger market may not always correspond to a more profitable business. When the market size is large, more competitors enter the industry, which eventually drives down the otherwise highly profitable pie of each player (this aspect of competition shall be discussed later in the book). Nevertheless, the market size is a good indicator of the demand for goods.

d. **Availability and price of alternatives:** The availability and price of alternative goods are a big factor in determining the demand. The alternative good could be of two types. The first type of alternative good is called a *substitute*. Substitutes are defined as two goods for which an increase in the price of one leads to an increase in the demand for the other. It is important to note here that goods with a high degree of substitutability are those that have a low *switching cost* for consumers. The switching cost is a type of transaction cost that the consumer will incur when they are switching from one good to another. An example of two substitute goods are burgers from McDonald's and Burger King.

The second form of an alternative good is called a *complement*. Complements are defined as two goods for which an increase in the price of one leads to a decrease in the demand for the other. For example, blades and razors are complementary goods. Substitutes and complements plays an important role in impacting the demand for a particular good. If Burger King raised the price of burgers, it would lose customers to McDonald's. Thus, if the price of a substitutable good increases, the demand for the original good increases. For complements, if the price of the complementary good increases, the demand for the original good decreases. For example, if the price of blades increases, people will stop purchasing razors from that particular brand.

The above four factors are responsible for a change in the demand for goods. Thus, for a given price, if any of the above factors change, the effect will be a change in demand. Figure 2.2 below lists the changes.

Figure 2.2 Factors affecting the change in demand

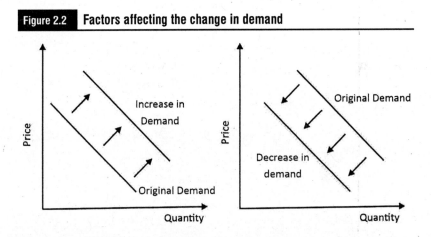

It is important to understand the difference between a *change in quantity demanded and a change in demand*. When price is the determining variable of change, the result is a change in quantity demanded. On the other hand, when any other factor apart from price changes, it is termed as the *change in demand*. Let us consider an example to clarify this point. Assume that you have an income of $100. For $10 per egg, you can buy 10 eggs. When the price increases to $20 per egg, you can only buy five eggs. Thus, with the same income, the change in quantity demanded is $10 - 5 = 5$

units. This is termed as the change in quantity demanded, which is represented by a movement along the demand curve. Now, assume that the price remains $10 per egg, but your income has increased from $100 to $200. Now, you can purchase 20 eggs. Thus, at the same price level, the demand has increased from 10 to 20 eggs, which is an increase of 10 eggs. This is termed the *change in demand*, which is represented by a rightward shift of the demand curve (Figure 2.3)

Figure 2.3   **Change in quantity demanded versus change in demand**

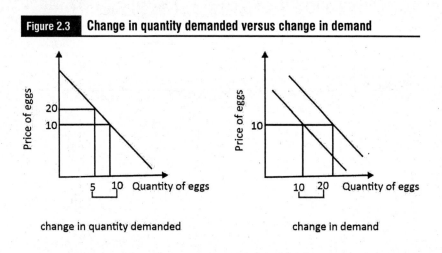

change in quantity demanded   change in demand

2.2.2 Supply curve

The supply curve of a good is the relationship between the price of a good and the quantity of the good that is supplied. [9] The supply curve illustrates how the quantity supplied changes when the price of goods changes. There is a positive association between price and quantity supplied, such that when the price increases, the quantity supplied increases, *ceteris paribus*. Why is this the case? As the price of goods increases, firms are incentivized to produce more, as the profits that they can generate from sales of more goods increase.

---

9. Mankiw, "Principles of Economics", 7th Edition

Figure 2.4 illustrates the relationship between price and supply. At price p_1, the quantity supplied is q_1. As the price increases p_2, the quantity supplied increases too q_2. Thus, there is a direct relationship between price and quantity supplied.

Figure 2.4 **Supply curve**

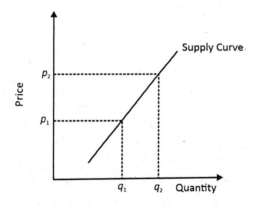

There are various factors that affect the supply decision of a producer. Some of the factors that significantly affect supply decisions are:

a. **Price of inputs:** The price of the input material is a significant factor that affects the supply decision for a producer. When the price of input material increases, the cost of goods increases. For a given market price, this increased cost of production lowers profitability, and hence the supply curve shifts to the left (see Figure 2.4). On the contrary, when the prices of inputs fall, the cost of production declines. For a given market price, this lowered cost of production increases profitability and shifts the supply curve to the right. As an example, if the cost of semiconductor chips decreases, the price of automobiles will decline, as semiconductor chips are a vital component of automobile vehicles. This will shift the supply curve of cards to the right.

b. **Increased use of technology:** An increase in the use of technology can improve the productivity of the firm, leading to a higher supply. Firms that are leveraging technology to scale production will be able to increase supply, compared to those that do not.

c. **Government policies:** Government policies can have a huge impact on the production and supply decisions of a firm. The two broad government policies that are applicable to firms are *taxes* and *subsidies*. A tax on production is a cost to the company as it increases its cost of production. For a given price point, a higher tax would result in a higher cost, resulting in a lower supply of the good. Hence, the supply curve would shift to the left (see Figure 2.5). On the contrary, a subsidy (also commonly known as a negative tax) is a gift to the firm as it lowers the cost of production. For a given price, this will increase the supply, thereby shifting the supply curve to the right.

d. **Future expectations:** If there are certain futuristic trends emerging, firms will increase supply to cater to the future market. For instance, while electric vehicle adoption is still at its nascent stage in many countries, firms that have a higher futuristic expectation that the market will grow will increase their production capacity to be future market leaders.

Figure 2.5 illustrates the changes in the supply curve for changes in parameters apart from price. Panel A lists out the factors that

lead to the increase in supply (rightward shift of the supply
curve). Panel B, on the right, lists out the factors that lead to the
decrease in the supply (leftward shift of the supply curve).

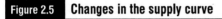

Figure 2.5   **Changes in the supply curve**

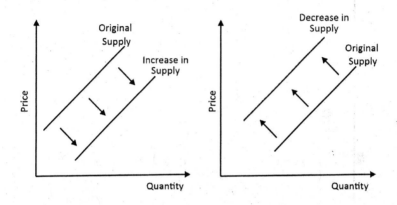

It is important to understand the difference between a *change in
quantity supplied* and a *change in supply*. When the price of goods
changes, the result is a change in the quantity supplied. On the
other hand, when any other factor apart from price changes, it
is termed as a *change in supply*. In other words, for a change in
quantity supplied, we move along the same supply curve, while
for a change in supply, the entire supply curve shifts.

2.3 Equilibrium in the Market

Market equilibrium is the region where the buyers' and sellers' needs are met. It is the point where the demand and supply forces meet. The demand and supply are both a function of price. Hence, the market equilibrium is the intersection of the demand and supply forces which produces a price point at which the goods are transacted in the market. Mathematically, the equilibrium is defined as:

$$Q_d\ (p) = Q_s\ (p)$$

$Q_d\ (p)$: the demand function of the good

$Q_s\ (p)$: the supply function of the good

Therefore, when the demand and the supply forces meet, the market price is determined. Figure 2.6 represents the demand and supply function of a market. The demand curve is downward-sloping, while the supply curve is upward-sloping. Price is measured on the vertical axis and quantity on the horizontal axis. At a low price p_2, the demand is very high (q_{d2}), however, the supply is very low (q_{s2}). Hence, the gap between the demand and supply is large (A-B). As the price rises, the gap between the demand and supply reduces. Finally, at price p^*, the price is in equilibrium (point E). This is the price at which both the buyer and the seller are willing to engage.

What happens at a price higher than p^*? At prices p_1, the supplier is willing to produce and sell q_{s1}, however, the demand for goods is very low (d). Hence, the gap again starts to increase (C-D). Thus, the market equilibrium is defined at a price p^*.

Figure 2.6   **Market equilibrium**

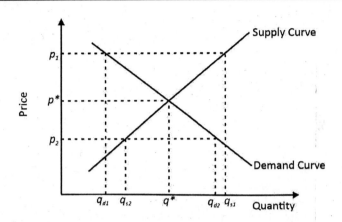

2.4 Comparative Statics

Having understood the mechanism through which price is determined in the market, it is important to examine what causes these price changes in a market. The price of a commodity is rarely static. Price is a dynamic variable that keeps changing based on a variety of factors. The mechanisms through which the price of goods is determined are known as comparative statics. Comparative statistics is essentially the study of price movements that are caused due to shifts in the demand and supply forces. Prices can move upwards or downwards due to the following reasons:

2.4.1 Upward movement of price

a. **Demand for the good increases, and supply remains constant**
It is often seen that during peak hours (morning office hours), the price of cab fares starts to surge. This is what is famously called surge pricing. [10] During peak office hours, the demand for cabs invariably increases. This causes the demand curve to shift up, resulting in an increase in prices.

b. **Supply for the good decreases, demand remains constant**
Reduction in supply can lead to an increase in price. For instance, in oil markets, unforeseen circumstances cause disruptions in the supply leading to higher prices.

2.4.2 Downward movement of price

a. **Demand for the good falls, supply remains constant**
The price of goods can fall if the demand for goods declines, in spite of the supply remaining constant. In such a scenario, there is a huge inventory that is accumulated by the firm, and the price of the produce falls.

b. **Supply of the good increases, demand remains constant**
The price of goods can decline if the supply is too high, while the demand does not change. As an example, if Apple produces too many phones of a particular version, but there is no demand for it, the price of the good will start to drop, and Apple will have to sell it for a lower price.

---

10. In many countries, the government has put a cap on surge pricing by limiting the upper price that can be charged to customers.

2.5 Are Price Movements Always Unambiguous?

While the above cases lead to an unambiguous change in the direction of the price, there are cases and scenarios where the price movement is ambiguous. This occurs when both the demand and the supply factors move together. The following cases illustrate the cases of ambiguous price movements.

a. **Demand for the good increases, and supply of the good increases**

When the demand for goods increases, the price tends to move upwards. However, if the supply of goods is increased, that pushes the price downwards. Hence the final price change will be a result of the dominating force between supply and demand. For instance, if the increase in demand exceeds the increase in supply, then the resulting price will increase. On the contrary, if the increase in supply exceeds the increase in demand, the resulting price will decline.

b. **Demand for the good decreases, and the supply of the good decreases**

In a scenario where the demand for goods decreases, the price will see a downward movement. However, if the supply of goods starts to decline too, the price will start to move upwards. Hence, the final price will converge at a point depending on the dominating force between the decrease in supply versus the decrease in demand. If the fall in supply dominates, the fall in demand, then the price would rise. If the fall in demand exceeds the fall in supply, the price would fall.

Table 2.2 lists out the changes in quantity and price, whenever there are changes in either demand, supply, or both. It describes how prices and quantity change for every possible scenario of change in demand or supply.

Table 2.2	**Comparative statistics of changes in demand and supply**

	Constant Supply	Increase in Supply	Decrease in Supply
Constant Demand	Initial Equilibrium	• Price Decreases • Quantity Increases	• Price Increases • Quantity Decreases
Increase in Demand	• Price increases • Quantity increases	• Price increase or decrease • Quantity increases	• Price Increases • Quantity increase or decrease
Decrease in Demand	• Price decreases • Quantity decreases	• Price decreases • Quantity increase or decrease	• Quantity decreases • Price increase or decrease

2.6 Conclusion

This chapter explains the concepts of demand and supply and the role they play in the functioning of the market. It describes the factors that affect both demand and supply and how the market equilibrium price is reached. Finally, the chapter also describes the factors that lead to dynamic price movements and the role that demand and supply play in price adjustments.

Quiz

1. A market is a place where _____ and _____ meet.

    a. Buyers; suppliers

    b. Consumers; producers

    c. Households; firms

    d. All of the above

2. A marketplace can be in a physical form as well as an online marketplace.

    a. True

    b. False

    c. Cannot be determined

3. The demand curve is _____ to price.

    a. Positively related

    b. Negatively related

    c. Not related

    d. Both a and b

4. **The supply curve is _____ related to price.**

   a. Positively

   b. Negatively

   c. Not

   d. Both a and b

5. **At a price below the equilibrium price, the quantity demanded is _____ the quantity supplied.**

   a. Greater than

   b. Lesser than

   c. Equal to

   d. Both a and b

6. **At a price higher than the equilibrium price, the quantity demanded is _____ the quantity supplied.**

   a. Greater than

   b. Lesser than

   c. Equal to

   d. Both a and b

7. **At the equilibrium price, _____ is equal to _____.**

   a. Price; quantity

   b. Price; zero

   c. Quantity; one

   d. Demand; supply

8. **The factors affecting the change in demand are** _____.

   a. Income

   b. Taste and Preferences

   c. Availability of substitutes and complements

   d. All of the above

9. **The factors affecting the change in supply are** _____.

   a. Price of inputs

   b. Government policies

   c. Both a and b

   d. None of the above

10. **A simultaneous increase in demand and supply causes an** _____ **change in quantity, and an** _____ **change in price.**

   a. Ambiguous; unambiguous

   b. Unambiguous; ambiguous

   c. Ambiguous; ambiguous

   d. Unambiguous; unambiguous

Answers	1 – d	2 – a	3 – b	4 – a	5 – a
	6 – b	7 – d	8 –d	9 – c	10 – b

Chapter Summary

◆ Markets are defined as places where buyers and sellers meet.

◆ The market is a function of the demand and supply forces.

◆ The demand curve is downward sloping and is inversely related to price.

◆ The supply curve is upward-sloping and positively related to price.

◆ The equilibrium price in the market is the point where the demand and supply forces meet.

◆ The factors affecting the demand curve are market size, income, taste and preferences, and price of alternative goods.

◆ The factors affecting the supply curve are the price of inputs, increased use of technology, and the change in government policies, such as tax and subsidies.

Chapter **3**

Elasticity And Price Controls

This chapter deals with elasticity and the importance of price elasticity of demand. The chapter also discusses how government regulations can have an effect on the market forces and elasticities of goods or services.

The key learning objectives of this chapter include the reader's understanding of the following:

- The driving forces behind the demand and supply conditions in a market
- How elasticity impacts pricing
- Evaluating the effect of market forces under different degrees of elasticity
- Applying the principles of elasticity to real-life economic scenarios
- Evaluating the effect of government regulations on market forces

3.1 Elasticity

How would consumers respond if the price of gasoline increased by \$2? How would producers respond if corporate taxes were to increase by five percent? The answers to these questions lie in a concept called **elasticity**. The price elasticity of demand measures the sensitivity of the quantity demanded to price. [11] Elasticity is an important concept related to the demand and supply of goods. In simple terms, elasticity is the percentage change in quantity demanded or percentage change in quantity supplied, divided by the percentage change in price. It is represented by the notation $\in$.

$$\in = \frac{\% \ change \ in \ quantity}{\% \ change \ in \ price} = \frac{\left(\frac{\Delta Q}{Q}\right)}{\left(\frac{\Delta P}{P}\right)} = \left(\frac{\Delta Q}{\Delta P}\right)\left(\frac{P}{Q}\right)$$

The value of $\in$ can either be greater than, less than, or equal to 1. If the value is equal to 1, the good is said to be *unit elastic*. If this value is less than 1, the good is termed to be *inelastic*. On the other hand, if the value is greater than 1, the good is termed to be *elastic*. Let us now look at the elasticity of demand and the elasticity of supply of goods.

3.1.1 Elasticity of demand

The quantity demanded for a particular good is inversely related to its price. However, a more pertinent question would be: By how much? By how much does the quantity demanded change, whenever there is a one percent change in the price of the

---

11. *Microeconomics*, David Besanko and Ronald Braeutigam (6th Edition)

good? The price elasticity of demand is a ratio of the percentage change in the quantity demanded over the percentage change in the price of a good or service. [12] For instance, assume that the price of eggs increases by two percent a particular year. However, the quantity demanded of eggs decreased by four percent. The elasticity is two. Since the value is greater than one, the market is said to be highly elastic.

$$Price\ Elasticity\ of\ Demand = \frac{Percentage\ change\ in\ quantity\ demanded}{Percentage\ change\ in\ price}$$

$$Price\ Elasticity\ of\ Demand = \frac{4}{2}\ 2$$

High elasticity implies that if prices continue to increase, the consumption of eggs will decline even further. On the other hand, if the price of eggs increases by two percent leading to a one percent decline in the quantity demanded, the elasticity is then 0.5. The market for eggs is said to be inelastic in this case. This implies that even as prices increase, the consumption of eggs does not decline in the same proportion as the increase in price.

3.1.2 Elasticity of supply

The supply of a good has a positive correlation with the price of the good. The elasticity of supply is the degree of the change in quantity supplied due to a change in the price of the good. For example, if the price of eggs increases by two percent, and the quantity supplied increases by four percent, then the elasticity of

12. Dean, Erik, Justin Elardo, Mitch Green, Benjamin Wilson, and Sebastian Berger. *Principles of Economics*. Open Oregon Educational Resources, 2016. https://openoregon. pressbooks.pub.

supply is (4/2) = 2. Since this is greater than 1, the market is said to be highly elastic in nature.

$$Price\ Elasticity\ of\ Supply = \frac{Percentage\ change\ in\ quantity\ supplied}{percentage\ change\ in\ price}$$

On the other hand, if the price of eggs increases by two percent, and the quantity supplied increases by only one percent, then the elasticity of supply is 0.5, and the market is said to be inelastic in nature. Table 3.1 provides a summary list of the degree of elasticity under different conditions.

Table 3.1 **Relationship between price, quantity, and elasticity**

Price	Sign	Demand/Supply	Result
% Change in price	>	% Change in quantity demanded (supplied)	Highly inelastic
% Change in price	=	% Change in quantity demanded (supplied)	Unit elastic
% Change in price	<	% Change in quantity demanded (supplied)	Highly elastic

3.2 Factors Affecting Elasticity

What determines the degree of elasticity of a good? How does one understand whether a particular good is highly elastic or inelastic? There are several factors that affect the elasticity of goods, which are as follows:

a. **Availability of substitutes:** If a particular good does not have many substitutes available, and is also necessary for consumption, that good is said to be highly inelastic. A good example of an inelastic good is healthcare. An emergency health operation or a life-saving drug is a perfect example of an inelastic good that the consumer will purchase irrespective of the price in order to save their life. On the other hand, if a good has a large variety of substitutes, then the good is termed to be highly elastic. For example, if Pepsi increases the price of its drink, then consumers will switch to Coke. It is also important to note here that the switching cost plays a crucial role in determining the elasticity of the good. If the tastes of Coke·and Pepsi are very different, then the switching cost for the consumer becomes high, and each good will then be relatively inelastic. However, if the taste is similar, then the switching cost is low, leading to each one being highly elastic.

b. **Time horizon:** Time affects the elasticity of a good. Certain goods are more elastic in the short run, but relatively inelastic in the long run. For instance, the demand for energy consumption is inelastic in the short run, but relatively elastic in the long run. As the cost of electricity increases, consumers will be unable to change their consumption patterns overnight. However, in the long run (in due course of time), consumers might switch to more efficient products that consume less electricity, thereby becoming elastic in the long run. Time plays a crucial role even in the elasticity of supply for producers.

3.3 Perfectly Elastic and Inelastic Demand and Supply

It has been established that if the percentage change in quantity is higher than the percentage change in price, then the good is said to be highly elastic. On the other hand, if the percentage change in quantity is lower than the percentage change in price, the good is said to be inelastic. This applies to both demand and supply. However, an extreme case also exists when there is perfect elasticity (inelasticity) for both demand and supply.

3.3.1 Perfectly elastic and inelastic demand

A perfectly elastic demand curve is illustrated by a horizontal demand curve, with price on the vertical axis, and quantity on the horizontal axis. This implies that for any change in supply, there is no change in price, but only a change in quantity demanded (see Panel A of Figure 3.1). On the other hand, a perfectly inelastic demand curve is a completely vertical demand curve, with price on the vertical axis, and quantity on the horizontal axis. This implies that any change in supply will result only in a change in price and not quantity (Panel B of Figure 3.1).

Figure 3.1 **Perfectly elastic and inelastic demand curves**

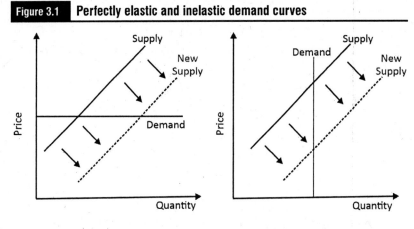

A: Perfectly Elastic Demand Curve   B: Perfectly Inelastic Demand Curve

3.3.2 Perfectly elastic and inelastic supply

A perfectly elastic supply curve is illustrated by a completely horizontal supply curve, with price on the vertical axis, and quantity supplied on the horizontal axis. This implies that for any change in demand, there is no change in price, but only a change in quantity supplied (see Panel A of Figure 3.2). On the other hand, a perfectly inelastic supply curve is a completely vertical supply curve, with price on the vertical axis, and quantity on the horizontal axis. This implies that any change in demand will result only in a change in price and not quantity (Panel B of Figure 3.2).

Figure 3.2   **Perfectly elastic and inelastic supply curves**

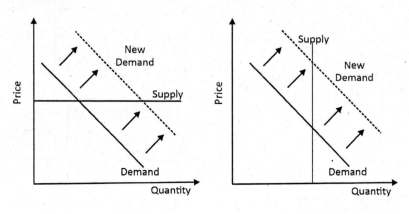

A: Perfectly Elastic Supply   B: Perfectly Inelastic Supply

3.4 Cross-Price Elasticity of Demand and Supply

Till this point, the focus was on the own-price elasticity of demand and supply. Simply put, the elasticity was determined depending on the relationship between price and quantity for the *same good*. The cross-price elasticity of demand and supply is defined as the percentage change in quantity demanded (or supplied) by the percentage change in price of another good. It is denoted as:

$$\epsilon_{12} = \frac{Percentage\ change\ in\ quantity\ demand\ (or\ supplied)\ of\ good\ 1}{percentage\ change\ in\ price\ of\ good\ 2}$$

When two goods are related to each other, the elasticity between them is termed **cross-price** elasticity. Both goods can either be substitutes or complements of each other. Substitutes are those goods that have the same level of utility to the consumer.

Complements are those goods that have to be used in conjunction with one another. How does the cross-price elasticity differ for substitutes and complements? The intuitive understanding is the following: Assume that two goods are substitutes. If the price of one good increases, the consumer will immediately purchase the other good at a lower price. Thus, the cross-price elasticity for substitutable goods is positive. (the numerator and the denominator increase). On the other hand, if two goods are complements in nature, then as the price of one good increases, the quantity demanded for the other good will decline as both goods are used together. Therefore, the cross-price elasticity for complements is negative (the numerator increases, but the denominator declines).

3.5 Market Failures and Price Mechanisms

While market forces are the best determinants of market prices, they can sometimes lead to the distortion of economic welfare in certain cases. For example, during a particular season of unforeseen weather changes, the prices of fruits and vegetables could increase drastically, following which lower-income households will not be able to purchase food. Therefore, to ensure equity in access, the governments intervene to set the price such that access is equitable. A popular example where market intervention by the government takes place is surge pricing in ride-hailing companies, such as Uber. The government limits the price by setting a cap beyond which companies cannot raise prices even during peak hours. The two popular mechanisms by which the government intervenes in the market are (a) price floors and (b) price ceilings

3.5.1 Price floor

A price floor is a minimum price below which the price cannot fall. It is also called a minimum support price. In the 1980s, the United States Department of Agriculture practiced the policy of a minimum support price for dairy farmers. In essence, it meant that the dairy farmers were assured of a minimum price for their produce. However, the policy was not very useful, as it led to a loss of government revenue in the long run. Panel B of Figure 3.3 illustrates the economic effect of a price floor. The initial market equilibrium is at p^*. The price floor is determined at p_1. At p_1, the demand is higher than the supply, causing a surplus of q_2-q_1 units. As the price floor reduces towards the equilibrium price, the surplus reduces.

3.5.2 Price ceiling

A price ceiling is a maximum binding price above which the price cannot be increased further. A good example to understand the application of a price ceiling is the practice of rent controls in the United States. Following World War II, America practiced rent control on the housing economy. However, this policy was slowly abandoned because rent controls were deterring builders from building new homes, as homeowners had little incentive to purchase a home.

Panel A of Figure 3.3 illustrates the economic effect of a price ceiling. The initial market equilibrium is at p^*. The price floor is determined at p_2. At p_2, the demand is higher than the supply, causing a shortage of q_2 - q_1 units. As the price ceiling increases towards the equilibrium price, the shortage accordingly reduces.

Figure 3.3 **Price ceiling and price floor mechanisms**

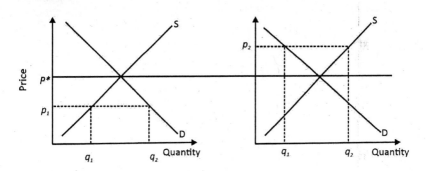

3.6 Market Implications of Elasticity

Is a high degree of elasticity good for the market? Do consumers benefit from goods and services that are highly elastic or relatively inelastic? How do producers benefit from the degree of elasticity of these products? These questions are critical in understanding the implications of the elasticity of products for different stakeholders in the economy. The answer to these depends on the direction of price changes. Take, for example, a change in the price of gasoline, which is an inelastic market. When the price of gasoline increases, consumers have no option but to pay the higher price. Using public transportation will be costlier too due to the price hike. Hence, producers of oil benefit immensely from an increase in price in a highly inelastic market.

However, assume that the price of gasoline witnessed a decline. Will individuals consume more of it, just because the price has fallen? People will not travel more just because there is a decline in oil prices. Hence, producers do not benefit when prices fall in an inelastic market. Now, consider the market for bread.

This is a relatively elastic market, as individuals can shift to other food items if the price of bread increases. Being highly elastic, if the price increases, the producers do not benefit, as consumers immediately shift to other options. However, when prices decrease, consumers will want to consume more of it. Hence, producers enjoy a higher revenue due to greater volume. Thus, producers and consumers benefit under a price decline or a price rise, depending on the elasticity of the market. Table 3.2 illustrates this perfectly.

Table 3.2   **Elasticity changes and market implications**

		Price	
		Increases	**Decreases**
	Elastic	Consumers *gain*	Consumers *gain*
		Producers *lose*	Producers *gain*
Elasticity			
	Inelastic	Consumers *lose*	Consumers *gain*
		Producers *gain*	Producers *lose*

Quiz

1. If the percentage increase in price is less than the percentage decrease in quantity demanded, the good is said to be highly___.

   a. Elastic

   b. Inelastic

   c. Perfectly elastic

   d. Perfectly inelastic

2. If the percentage increase in price is higher than the percentage increase in quantity supplied, the good is said to be _____.

   a. Elastic

   b. Inelastic

   c. Unit elastic

   d. Perfectly inelastic

3. The cross-price elasticity for substitutes is _____.

   a. Positive

   b. Negative

   c. Zero

   d. Cannot be determined

4. **When demand is perfectly elastic, an increase in supply causes quantity to ____ and price to ____.**

   a. Increase; decrease

   b. Decrease; increase

   c. Increase; remain constant

   d. Decrease; remain constant

5. **When demand is perfectly inelastic, a decrease in supply causes quantity to ____ and price to ____.**

   a. Remain constant; increase

   b. Increase; remain constant

   c. Decrease; remain constant

   d. Remain constant; decrease

6. **When supply is perfectly inelastic, an increase in demand causes quantity to ____ and price to ____.**

   a. Remain constant; decrease

   b. Remain constant; increase

   c. Increase; remain constant

   d. Decrease; remain constant

7. **A price ceiling causes a _____.**

    a. Shortage of goods

    b. Surplus of goods

    c. Decline in demand

    d. None of the above

8. **A price floor causes a _____.**

    a. Surplus of goods

    b. Shortage of goods

    c. Change in supply

    d. None of the above

9. **The lower the price floor towards equilibrium, the _____ the _____.**

    a. Lower; surplus

    b. Lower; shortage

    c. Higher; surplus

    d. Higher; shortage

10. Assume that there is a drought in a region, causing the agricultural output of rice to decline. This causes an increase in the price of rice. However, the demand for rice remains the same. Thus, rice is an _____ product.

    a. Inelastic

    b. Elastic

    c. Perfectly elastic

    d. None of the above

Answers	1 – a	2 – b	3 – a	4 – c	5 – a
	6 – b	7 – a	8 –a	9 – a	10 – a

Chapter Summary

◆ Elasticity is defined as the percentage change in quantity demanded (or supplied) by the percentage change in price.

◆ The value of the elasticity can range from <1 (inelastic) to >1 (elastic).

◆ Elasticity is a function of the availability of substitutes and the time period.

◆ Two extreme cases of elasticity are perfect elasticity and perfect inelasticity.

◆ Cross-price elasticity is positive for substitutes and negative for complements.

◆ Governments intervene in the market to correct prices in order to increase economic and social welfare.

◆ Two forms of market interventions are price ceilings and price floors.

◆ Price ceiling is a mechanism by which an upper limit on the price is set. The market price is not allowed to increase above this specified ceiling.

◆ Price floor is a mechanism by which a minimum specified limit is set on the price. The market price cannot go below this limit.

CASE STUDY

1. Trends in Gasoline Prices

Quarterly household expenditures for gasoline and estimated gallons of gasoline purchased, 2004-2014

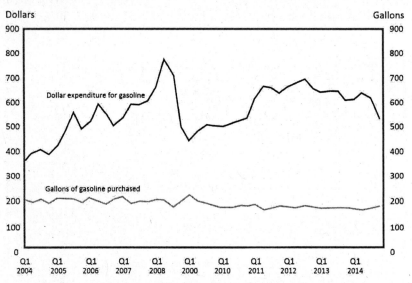

Note: Dollar expenditures for gasoline include out-of-town trips and everyday use from the Consumer Expenditure Survey. Calculations for the estimated gallons of gasoline purchased use Consumer Price Index Data.

Source: U.S Burea-u of Labor Statistics

The law of supply and demand dictates that consumers should reduce their purchases when prices of goods rise. According to Graph 3.1, the estimated gallons purchased by a household have remained rather constant each quarter over the past 11 years. [13] As spending on gasoline (including out-of-town trips) has climbed

13. Crain, Eliana Eitches and Vera. "Using Gasoline Data to Explain Inelasticity : Beyond the Numbers: U.S. Bureau of Labor Statistics." https://www.bls.gov

due to gasoline prices rising, one would believe that it would lead to households purchasing less. However, that is not the trend being displayed and as gasoline prices increased, spending on gasoline also increased. The expectation is that as the price per gallon rises, a corresponding decline in demand for gasoline will occur.

Discussion Question:

What could be the possible factors for this trend?

2. The application of elasticity of demand for US Airlines[14]

Major U.S. airlines are expected to reiterate the strength of travel demand when earnings season gets underway later this week. But with rising interest rates, high inflation, mounting job losses and turmoil in the banking industry increasing the odds of an economic recession, the spotlight will be on the elasticity of consumer demand. Pent-up travel demand as well as constrained airline capacity due to shortages of aircraft, spare parts, and labor have, thus far, allowed the industry to avoid the fallout from a slowdown in the broader economy.
The question remains how long this travel boom will last.

"The fallout from the recent banking turmoil and rising interest rates does in our view skew risk to the downside," said Christopher Stathoulopoulos, an analyst at Susquehanna Financial Group.

---

14. Singh, Rajesh Kumar. "Elasticity of Travel Demand in Focus as U.S. Carriers Report Earnings." Reuters, April 11, 2023, sec. Aerospace & Defense. https://www.reuters.com

Chief executives of major carriers last month rushed to reassure jittery investors after a profit warning from United Airlines (UAL.O) stoked worries about the industry's pricing power. The industry has been leaning on soaring consumer demand to mitigate higher labor and fuel costs with higher fares.

Yet, Delta Air Lines (DAL.N), which kicks off the earnings season on Thursday, has said its first-quarter earnings would suffer due to a run-up in operating costs after its new contract deal with pilots. The Atlanta-based carrier is expected to report a profit of 30 cents a share.

Chicago-based United, which is due to report its first-quarter result next week, is tipped to post a loss of 66 cents a share due to higher costs from a potential contract deal with pilots.

Analysts at Moody's Investors Service estimate labor expense for U.S. carriers will increase by 19% this year. Meanwhile, surprise output cuts by OPEC+ oil producers earlier this month are expected to drive up fuel bills for airlines, hurting their profits.

"The price elasticity of demand over economic cycles will be the ultimate arbiter of the industry's ability to cover increasing costs," Moody's said.

Discussion Question:

Comment on how airline pricing and demand in this context are linked to the elasticity of consumer demand.

Chapter 4

Consumer Behavior

This chapter deals with consumer choice and behavior. Understanding consumer choices and consumer behavior is critical for various stakeholders in an economy. In this chapter, we are going to explore what are the salient features of consumer behavior, and how consumer behavior can be applied to markets.

The key learning objectives of this chapter include the reader's understanding of the following:

- The basic tenets of consumer behavior

- The role of budget and preferences in consumer choices

- Applying the principles of marginal analysis to consumer decision-making

- Evaluating consumer equilibrium using the principles of marginal analysis

4.1 The Budget Constraint

Constraints are central to understanding consumer behavior. The budget constraint is the maximum amount of money that the consumer has and is willing to spend on different goods and services. One of the ten principles of economics states that consumers face trade-offs. In other words, if they consume a particular amount of one good, they will have to sacrifice a particular amount of the other good. The underlying principle is based on the budget constraint that the consumer faces. Let us try to understand this with an example.

Assume Bob has $10 to spend. He visits the grocery store and likes two items–(a) A can of Coke; and (b) a jar of cookies. The can of Coke costs him $2, and the jar of cookies costs him $2. Therefore, Bob has the following choices as illustrated in Table 4.1. He can purchase one unit of Coke and four units of cookies, two units of Coke and three units of cookies, and so on and so forth.

Table 4.1	The Budget Constraint

Units of Coke	Units of Cookies	Amount Spent
1	4	$10
2	3	$10
5	0	$10
3	2	$10
4	1	$10

Bob can choose from each of these choices depending on the satisfaction that he derives. Here, we assume that the entire amount is utilized, and there are no savings. Of course, in reality, Bob might purchase one can of Coke and one jar of cookies and save the remaining $6. However, the assumption of no savings makes it easier to understand this concept.

Figure 4.1 illustrates the budget line for Bob. Bob can choose any point within the budget constraint, as shown in the triangle in the figure. The boundary conditions are marked by the respective intercepts. For instance, if Bob were to choose only Coke, he could purchase five units, while if he were to purchase only cookies, he could purchase five units. The budget line is mathematically denoted as:

$$p_1 x_1 + p_2 x_2 \le M$$

p_1 = Price of good 1; p_2: price of good 2; x_1 : quantity of good 1; x_2: quantity of good 2; M: Income

Figure 4.1　The budget line

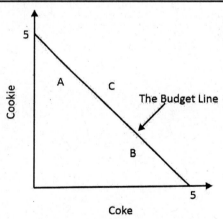

In other words, the consumer is constrained to choose any combination of Coke or cookies within the triangle. Any choice above the budget line is not a possibility for the consumer. Points

A and B are possible choices for the consumer, as they lie within the triangle. However, Point C, where the consumer probably wants to consume five units each of both goods is not possible, since it falls out of the budget line.

The slope of the budget line represents the opportunity cost or *the relative price* that the consumer faces. In this case, the slope of the line is 1 (price of coke/price of cookie jar). This implies that, for every unit of cookie that Bob gives up, he can buy an additional can of Coke. When the price of either of the goods changes, the slope of the line changes. For instance, if the price of Coke reduces to $1, while the price of cookies remains at $2, then Bob can consume either five units of cookies or 10 units of Coke. Notice how the total amount of coke consumed can be increased due to a fall in the price of coke. This pivots the budget line outwards. While the budget line is fixed at 5 units on the vertical axis, it moves to 10 units on the horizontal axis (Panel A of Figure 4.2). In a similar way, if the price of cookies fell to $1, while the price of Coke remained at $2, then the budget line would tilt outwards on the vertical axis, with Bob being able to consume 10 units of Coke and five units of cookies.

Figure 4.2	Price effects on the budget line

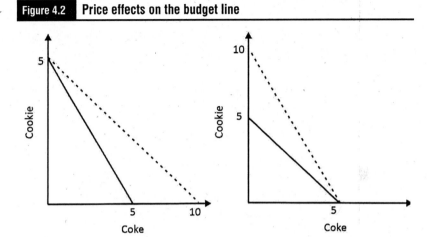

A: Decrease in the price of coke   B: Decrease in the price of cookie

4.1.1 Change in income level

We started by assuming that Bob has $10 to begin with. With coke and cookies costing $2 each, the possible options for Bob were listed in Table 1. Now, if we assume that Bob's income has increased by $10, such that his total income is now $20, he can purchase a higher amount of both goods. How is this increase in income represented graphically? Figure 4.3 shows the initial budget line when his income was $10. At the extreme levels, he could either use his income to purchase five units of Coke or 5 units of cookies. However, when his income increases by $10, Bob can now purchase 10 units of coke or 10 units of cookies. In other words, his consumption set has increased. This is illustrated by a rightward shift of the budget line. Conversely, if his income decreases to $2, then Bob can either purchase just one unit of Coke or one unit of cookies. In other words, his consumption set has been restricted. This is represented by a leftward shift of the budget line. Thus, an increase in income shifts the budget line outwards, while a decrease in income shifts the budget line inwards. It is important to note that this is a *parallel shift*. There is no change in the *slope* of the budget line, as the prices for both goods remain the same.

Even without an income change, the budget line can shift in a parallel manner. If the prices of both goods increase or decrease in the same proportion, it would result in a parallel shift in the budget line. Considering the same example, assume that the price of both a can of Coke and a jar of cookies reduces by $1, such that the price of both becomes $1 each. Then the slope of the budget line remains the same, and the budget line shifts outwards, with the 10 units on both axes ($1 x 10 units = $10).

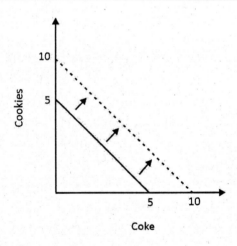

4.2 Consumer Preferences

In the previous section, we focused on the budget constraint which is the amount of money that limits the consumer's choice.

Bob could choose any of the five options laid out in Table 1, however, which choice Bob actually chooses depends on the level of satisfaction that he obtains when he consumes each of these combinations of goods. The level of satisfaction that the consumer gains while consuming goods is termed **utility**. While utility is hard to measure in real life, an approximate way of capturing utility is based on the **willingness to pay** for that resource. For example, if we assume that Bob prefers Coke over cookies, then he would be willing to pay much more for Coke than cookies. Therefore, if the price of Coke were to increase to $4, and cookies remain priced at $2, he would probably still choose more Coke over cookies.

4.2.1 Utility

Utility is broadly defined as the level of satisfaction that is derived from the consumption of a good. It is defined by the symbol U. The utility that a consumer receives depends on his taste and preferences for certain goods, and hence is very dynamic in nature.

An important concept in utility is called marginal utility (MU). **Marginal utility** is defined as the extra utility that the consumer gains by consuming an additional unit of the good. Mathematically, it is defined as MU $=\frac{\Delta U}{\Delta X}$ The concept of marginal utility is best explained in Table 4.2. Table 4.2 shows the corresponding utility obtained from consuming different units of the good. Marginal utility is defined as the additional change in utility gained by consuming an additional unit of the good. So, the marginal utility by consuming the second unit is (20-10) = 10. Similarly, the marginal utility obtained by consuming the third unit is (28-20) = 8.

Table 4.2	Illustration of utility and marginal utility based on consumption

Amount of goods consumed	Utility obtained	Marginal Utility
1	10	-
2	20	+10
3	28	+8
4	32	+4
5	34	+2
6	34	0
7	32	-2
-	28	-4

Table 4.2 points out an important feature of the marginal utility. The last column shows that as the amount of goods consumed increases, the extra utility that the consumer gains by consuming an additional unit *increases at a decreasing rate*. This is defined as **diminishing marginal utility**. Figure 4.4 shows the graph of the total utility and the marginal utility from consuming Good 1. The total utility has three sections. The first section is when utility increases as the amount of consumption of Good 1 increases. The second section is where the utility increases, *but at a decreasing rate*. The third section is where the utility declines after reaching its maximum. Marginal utility is linked to the total utility. Notice how the marginal utility continues to fall as the amount of goods consumed increases (Panel B on the right). The marginal utility reaches 0 (touches the horizontal axis) when the utility obtained is maximum. Point B on the horizontal axis (when MP = 0), corresponds to the same point when the total production has reached its maximum (TP = max; Panel A). Further to this point, the total utility starts to decline, and the marginal utility becomes negative.

Figure 4.4   **Total utility function and the marginal utility function**

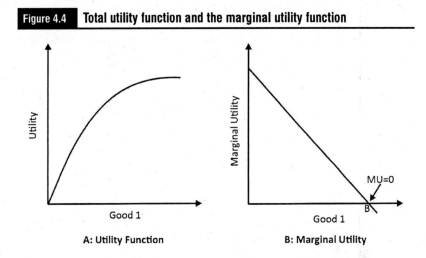

A: Utility Function   B: Marginal Utility

4.2.2 Indifference curves and the marginal rate of substitution

Indifference curves are a graphical way to represent the tastes and preferences of individuals. An indifference curve is a curve that illustrates the combination of different goods that the consumer can purchase (or consume) that provides the consumer with the same level of satisfaction. In other words, all combinations of goods on the same indifference curve provide the same level of utility to the consumer. Figure 4.5 illustrates the indifference curve for Bob. A jar of cookies is on the horizontal axis, while Coke is on the vertical axis.

Figure 4.5	A set of indifference curves

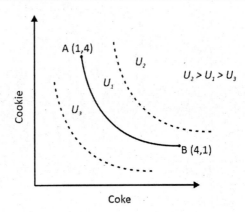

Point A on the indifference curve represents the basket of consumer preferences when Bob consumes one can of Coke and four jars of cookies. The budget spent is $10. Point B on the same indifference curve represents the point when Bob consumes four units of Coke and one jar of cookies, with the budget being $10. In both cases, the utility that Bob obtains is identically the same, and hence both these points are on the same indifference curve.

Why are indifference curves shaped in the fashion as illustrated in Figure 4.5? The reason for the curvilinear shape is attributed to the law of *diminishing marginal utility*. In other words, as the consumer moves from point A to point B, the consumer gives up fewer units of cookies to gain additional units of coke. Mathematically speaking, the slope of the indifference curve declines as we move from the top left to the bottom right. The slope of the indifference curve is defined as the **marginal rate of substitution**. Simply put, the marginal rate of substitution is the amount of one good that the consumer has to sacrifice in order to obtain one unit of the other good. You might wonder, who determines this sacrifice ratio? It is determined by the marginal utility of both goods. Thus, the slope of the indifference curve can also be written as $\dfrac{MU_1}{MU_2}$, where MU_1 is the marginal utility of good 1 and MU_2 is the marginal utility of good 2.

Slopes: The mathematics and economics of it

A slope is a mathematical concept which is defined as the change in y-coordinate to the change in the x-coordinate. Thus, if the y-coordinate changes faster than the x-coordinate, the slope increases. Conversely, if the x-coordinate changes faster than the y-coordinate, the slope diminishes.

From an economic point of view, slopes are essential to understand how utility, productivity, and preferences change. For example, in Figure 4,1, utility is measured on the y-axis and quantity on the x-axis. Thus, as quantity increases by one unit, utility increases. However, in the first section, utility increases by a larger extent than the change in quantity. In the second section, utility increases by a smaller extent than the change in quantity. Hence, in the first section the slope is larger than the slope in the second section. For indifference curves, as we move downwards from the top left, we see that the consumer has to give up lesser units of good on the y-axis, to get an additional unit of good on the x-axis. Hence, the slope is diminishing as we move down the indifference curve.

4.2.3 Shifts in the indifference curve

The indifference map is a set of indifference curves that provide different utility levels to the consumer. The indifference curve that is the farthest from the point of origin is the one that has the highest utility. Conversely, the indifference curve that is closest to the point of origin represents the lowest utility. When the consumer consumes more of both goods, thereby gaining a higher utility, the indifference curve shifts to the right (Figure 4.5). Conversely, when the consumer consumes less of both goods, there is a loss in overall utility, and the indifference curve shifts to the left. Thus, a leftward shift of the indifference curve implies a loss in utility, while a rightward shift implies a gain in utility. In other words, the rightmost indifference curve has the highest utility for the consumer, while the indifference curve closest to the origin has the lowest utility for the consumer.

Thus, while the level of utility is constant across an indifference curve, the level of utility differs as you move across indifference curves. Of course, consumers would like to be on the highest possible indifference curve. However, the actual point of consumption will be a function of both the budget constraint and the indifference curve. If the budget line is below a particular indifference curve, then consumers will be unable to achieve the level of utility obtained from that particular indifference curve.

4.3 Consumer Equilibrium

Now that the consumer has stated preferences, as well as the budget provided, the next stage would be to understand what would be the optimal point of consumption. This optimal point of consumption is often referred to as **consumer equilibrium.** Consumer equilibrium is defined as the point where the consumer receives the bang for the buck. Any consumer would want to maximize the utility that they receive from consuming products. However, they need to maximize this utility, subject to a constraint–which is the budget constraint.

How does the consumer understand what the best point of consumption is? Let us understand this through an example. Assume that the price of a cookie is $2 per unit, and the price of coke is $2 per unit. The marginal utility that the consumer gets from one unit of cookie is 10, while the marginal utility that the consumer gets from one unit of Coke is 20. Then, the marginal utility per price for good 1 is (10/2) = 5, while the marginal utility per price for good 2 is (20/2) = 10. Hence, the consumer will consume more of good 2 and less of good 1. As the consumption of good 2 increases, the marginal utility will start to decline (given the law of diminishing marginal utility), till a point where the ratio of the marginal utility by the price of the good remains the same for both. In this case, the consumer is indifferent between consuming either good 1 or good 2. Thus, the rule of thumb is that the consumer equilibrium will be met at the point where the consumer gets the *bang for the buck.* In other words, it is at the point where the ratio of the marginal utility to the price is the same across all goods.

Consumer equilibrium is attained when:

$$\frac{Marginal\ Utility\ of\ Good\ 1}{Price\ of\ Good\ 1} = \frac{Marginal\ Utility\ of\ Good\ 2}{Price\ of\ Good\ 2}$$

The ratio, of marginal utility to price can be thought of as the benefit-to-cost ratio that the consumer enjoys. The consumer will end up purchasing more of that good where the ratio of the marginal utility to price is higher.

4.4 Concluding Remarks and Practical Applications

As a reader, you are probably baffled after reading this chapter. You may be wondering—do all consumers really do all these calculations before they make their purchases? The simple answer is no. However, there is a back-of-the-envelope calculation that is close to the consumer decision-making theory. Most consumers actually perform this calculation while deciding how to consume. There are several real-life applications of consumer behavior. One good example of a real-life application of consumer behavior is described below:

4.4.1 Offers at retail stores

If you were to shop at popular retail chains, a popular offer that you would often see is: buy 2, get 10 percent off, buy 3, get 20 percent off. These offers are very popular, especially towards the end of a particular season. The principle that the retail chain is applying here is that of diminishing marginal utility.

The retail chain knows that it needs to get the items off the shelves. However, it is also aware of the fact that as a consumer purchases more of the same item, the marginal utility that the consumer gains begins to diminish. Hence, in order to match the diminishing marginal utility, the retail store starts to reduce the price, such that the ratio of the marginal utility to price is equalized. In this manner, retail stores apply this principle of consumer behavior to their business.

The principles of consumer behavior are crucial for both businesses and governments. It helps businesses and governments to understand how consumers react to different scenarios. This helps them in designing optimal offers and policies respectively. For instance, when a government decides between a cash transfer or an in-kind transfer for low-income households, it takes into account how the households will react to getting money (cash) versus goods (in-kind). Getting more of the same goods might lead to a lowering of utility; however, getting money in hand might give them the freedom to choose their own consumption basket. Therefore, understanding the nuances of consumer behavior is essential to business and government administration.

Quiz

1. **As a consumer increases the consumption of the same product, the utility _____.**

   a. Increases

   b. Decreases

   c. Remains the same

   d. Both a and b

2. **The marginal utility of a product _____ over time.**

   a. Decreases

   b. Increases

   c. Remains the same

   d. Both a and b

3. **Marginal utility is defined as the utility gained by consuming the ____ product over time.**

   a. Same

   b. Different

   c. One

   d. Both a and c

4. **All points on an indifference curve have _____ of utility to the consumer.**

   a. The same level

   b. Different levels

   c. No level

   d. None of the above

5. **The further the indifference curve is from the origin, the _____ is the utility.**

   a. Higher

   b. Lower

   c. Similar

   d. Neither a nor b

6. **The slope of the budget line is a ratio of the ____ of both goods.**

   a. Prices

   b. Quantity

   c. Prices and quantity

   d. Quality

7. The budget line shifts in a parallel manner when there is a change in the _____.

   a. Price of one good

   b. Price of both goods in the same proportion

   c. Income

   d. Both (b) and (c)

8. A higher indifference curve represents a _____ level of utility.

   a. Higher

   b. Lower

   c. Zero

   d. None of the above

9. The slope of the budget line is the ratio of _____.

   a. Quantities

   b. Prices

   c. Difference in prices

   d. Difference in quantities

10. Consumer equilibrium is met when the ratio of the marginal utilities is ____to the ratio of prices.

a. Equal

b. Less than equal

c. Higher than

d. None of the above

Answers	1 – a	2 – a	3 – a	4 – a	5 – a
	6 – a	7 – d	8 – a	9 – b	10 – a

Chapter Summary

◆ Consumer behavior deals with the decision-making principles of the consumer under a budget constraint and the preference level.

◆ The budget constraint is the amount of money the consumer has by which it purchases goods and services.

◆ Changes in the budget line are a function of a change in relative prices and a change in income.

◆ Change in relative prices changes the slope of the budget line, while change in income results in a shift in the budget line.

◆ Utility is defined as the amount of satisfaction that a consumer receives from a particular good.

◆ Marginal utility is defined as the additional utility gained by consuming an additional unit of the same good. Marginal utility decreases as the amount of goods consumed increases. This is termed diminishing marginal utility.

◆ An indifference curve is a graphical representation of the different combinations of goods that the consumer can consume at the same level of utility

◆ The higher the indifference curve, the higher the level of utility for the consumer.

◆ Consumer equilibrium is reached at the point where the ratio of the marginal utilities is equal to the ratio of the prices.

Chapter **5**

Theory of the Firm —Production

This chapter deals with the theory of the firm and the supply side of the market. It will focus on how firms behave, the factors that firms take into account while producing goods and services, and the mechanics behind the firm's production decision. This chapter will be the building framework to understand the supply curve of the industry.

Key learning objectives of this chapter include the reader's understanding of the following:

- The basic tenets of producer behavior

- The role of the production function in producer choice theory

- Evaluating the average and marginal product for a firm

- Analyzing the different types of return to scale

5.1 The Theory of the Firm

Why do firms exist? This question was answered by the famous Nobel Laureate Ronald Coase and other prominent economists such as Oliver Williamson. In his famous The Nature of the Firm written in the 1930s, Coase spoke about the *transaction costs* faced by firms, which define the boundary of the firm. What does transaction cost mean? Transaction costs are the costs that firms/people incur when they exchange goods and services with one another. Let us understand this through an example. Assume that a firm produces cars that they sell both in the domestic and international markets. The car manufacturer is also a steel manufacturer, which is an essential component of the car. The firm hires labor and invests in factories to produce both steel and cars. However, another important input for a car is semiconductors. The firm does not have the expertise to manufacture semiconductors. In other words, the transaction costs involved in setting up the research and design unit, hiring employees for the team, and creating semiconductors might be too costly, which will increase the overall cost of producing the car. It might be cheaper to source semiconductors from outside and utilize them for the car directly. Thus, the firm makes a trade-off by analyzing the transaction costs involved in manufacturing the parts of the car in-house versus buying it from outside. This is also known as the famous buy-or-own model in industrial economics. Thus, in this example, the boundary of the firm is now defined by the manufacturing of steel and cars. Transaction costs are important to both firms and individuals. Understanding what the relevant transaction costs in an activity are will lead to higher efficiency for firms and higher utility for consumers

5.2 The Production Function

The production function is the building block of the firm that eventually builds the supply curve of the market. The production function is a function of the inputs that the firm uses to produce the output. In a traditional sense, there are two basic units of production—labor and capital. The firm employs both these factors of production to produce the output. Labor refers to the manpower, while capital refers to the physical capital– the factories and machinery involved. Mathematically, the production function is denoted as:

$$q = f(L,K)$$

q is defined as the output at the firm level. L is the amount of labor employed, and K is the amount of capital employed.

5.2.1 Short-run and long-run production functions

The short-run and long-run production functions are divided based on a time horizon. Particularly, in the short run, one factor of production is kept fixed, while the other factor is variable. For instance, assume that the firm can employ more labor, but is unable to build more factories in the short run. Hence, capital is fixed, but labor is variable. In the long run, however, firms can increase both labor and capital, which increases the output at a much larger scale. The short-run production function is defined mathematically as:

$$q = f(L,\overline{K})$$

Here, $\overline{K}$ denotes that the level of capital is fixed for the firm. The only variable that is changing is labor. One important implication arises from the fact that one input of production is fixed. It is termed as the *law of variable proportion*. In short, the law states that as the amount of one input increases, given that the other input is fixed, the total product increases initially at an increasing rate, then at a decreasing rate, and further starts to decrease.

5.2.2 Marginal product

There is another important implication that arises due to the difference between the short and long run. This is defined as the marginal product. The *marginal product* is defined as the change in output due to a unit change in input.

Table 6.1 illustrates this concept well. The table shows that the amount of output produced increases at a decreasing rate, as the number of laborers increases. Why does this happen? In the short run, as the machinery and factories are fixed, any increase in labor will only lead to more laborers working on the same amount of machinery. Hence, the marginal product (the value added) by each individual worker will start to diminish.

Let us understand this through an example. Imagine that there is a restaurant that has a limited kitchen capacity. When the manager of the restaurant hires the first chef, he can produce 10 meals a day. When the manager hires the second chef, the total meals produced is 18, when the chef is hired, the total meals produced is 24. When the fourth chef is hired, the total meals produced remains 24, while when the fifth chef is employed, the output reduces to 22. What is the pattern that we notice here? As more chefs are hired, the value added by the additional next chef is lower than the previous chef. After a point, the value added by the next chef will be negative. The value added by the second chef is 8. The value added by the third chef is 6. The value added by the fourth chef is 0, while the value added by the last chef is -2.

Value added implies the marginal product of each chef. Why is this pattern observed? This is because the kitchen space is fixed, and the number of utensils that can be used is fixed. Hence, simply adding more chefs will not produce more meals, as now there are more hands doing the same job. In other words, the marginal product of labor starts to diminish and even becomes negative after a point in time. Table 5.1 illustrates the output and the marginal product from an additional unit of labor employed.

Table 5.1   **Input, output, and marginal product**

Labor Unit	Output	Marginal Product
1	10	-
2	18	+8
3	24	+6
4	24	0
5	22	-2

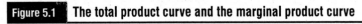

Figure 5.1 | **The total product curve and the marginal product curve**

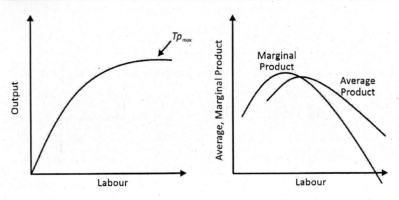

Look at Figure 5.1. The left panel (A) represents the production function of the firm. It increases initially at an increasing rate, then increases at a decreasing rate, and eventually declines. The marginal product curve, represented in the right panel (B), is derived from the production function. The marginal product, defined as the value added by the extra unit of input, increases first, and then starts to decline. The marginal product reaches the horizontal axis (marginal product = 0), when the total production function reaches its peak. In other words, the topmost point in panel A corresponds to the point where the marginal product curve touches the horizontal axis. Once the production function starts to decline, the marginal product becomes negative. Corresponding this to Table 5.1, the negative marginal product is seen as the labor increases from four to five units. At four units of labor, the firm has reached its optimal production.

5.3 Isoquants

Isoquants are the production-level counterpart of indifference curves. In essence, what an indifference curve is to a consumer, an isoquant is to a producer. An isoquant is a curve that represents the different combinations of inputs that can be used by the producer, which will yield the same level of output. The word isoquant is a combination of two words: iso (equal) plus quant (quantity). Thus, the curve that represents the possible input combinations for the producer that will produce the same level of output is termed an isoquant.

Table 5.2 illustrates this point clearly. A producer faces three choices. Choice A uses two units of labor and five units of capital, thereby producing 10 units of output. Choice B uses three units of labor and three units of capital, thereby producing 10 units of output. Lastly, choice C uses five units of labor and two units of capital, thereby producing 10 units of output. Hence, the producer can choose either of the options. This combination is represented in Figure 5.2.

Table 5.2	Input choices for a producer		
Choices	Labor (L)	Capital (K)	Output
A	2	5	10
B	3	3	10
C	5	2	10

Figure 5.2   **An isoquant map**

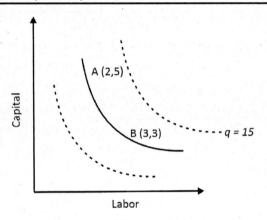

Figure 5.2 represents a typical isoquant which lists out the possible input choices for the same level of output (10 units).

The properties of an isoquant are very similar to an indifference curve. Isoquants are mostly curvilinear due to the property of diminishing marginal productivity. This implies that as the producer uses more of one input, he needs to give up less of the other input. Why is that so? Marginal productivity states that as the amount of one input increases, the output generated by that respective input increases at a decreasing rate. Given the diminishing marginal productivity rule, it does not make sense for the producer to sacrifice more of the other input. Hence, the producer gives up fewer quantities of one input to get an additional quantity of another input. This is the reason why the shape of the isoquant is curvilinear. If you were to map the slope of the line from the top left to the bottom right, you would notice that the slope (vertical axis by horizontal axis) decreases.

An isoquant map is a series of isoquants, such that isoquants that are away from the origin denote a higher level of output, while isoquants that are towards the origin denote a lower level of output. Thus, firms would want to be at an isoquant that is farthest away from the origin, and move further to the right as the organization grows (from q = 5 to q = 15). Can an organization choose which isoquant it wants to be on? The constraint to this choice is the cost function to the firm. We shall discuss this in-depth in the next chapter. However, the cost function is an important constraint to the firm, which is similar to the budget constraint for the consumer. Thus, while the firm would want to produce and move to a higher isoquant, the restraining force is the cost function that the firm faces.

5.4 Isoquants and Types of Inputs

There are certain cases where the shape of the isoquant may not be the way it is demonstrated in Figure 5.3. The two specific cases are when the inputs are either substitutes or complements.

a. **Substitutes:** Substitutable inputs are those where the producer gets the same output by choosing either of the two inputs. For example, assume that a firm can either use five units of labor or purchase a machine to do a particular task. In other words, the efficiency of five units of labor is equal to one unit of machine. These two inputs are termed substitutes to the factors of production. Typically, the firm would choose the input that comes at a lower cost, such that the output produced is more cost-effective. However, cost is just one short-term aspect that the firm looks for. There are various other factors that firms take into account while deciding the inputs, in spite of them being substitutes for each other. Technology has led to the automation of various jobs over the last decade. However, not all jobs have been automated. What does the shape of an isoquant look like for two inputs that are substitutes? Remember, the shape of an isoquant is determined by the law of diminishing marginal productivity. In the case of substitutes, the firm would have to give up the same proportion of one input to get the equivalent proportion of the other input (since they are substitutes). Hence, the isoquants are downward-sloping straight lines with the slope being constant throughout the isoquant (Figure 5.3 a).

b. **Complements:** Inputs that are complements to each other are those that need to be used together. For example, if every machine that the firm uses needs two workers to operate it, then the workers and the machine are complementary inputs. Any increase in the number of workers or machines without changing the other input proportionately will yield no result.

The shape of isoquants that deal with complementary inputs are L-shaped in structure. The reason for that is explained here. Look at Figure 5.3 b, when the firm uses 2 units of L and 1 unit of K, the firm produces 10 units. Any further increase in L, without increasing K will not increase output (we move horizontally on the isoquant). Similarly, any increase in K, without moving L, will not yield any additional output, and we will move along the vertical line. To move from 10 units of output to 20, the firm has to hire 2 additional workers and one additional machine. This will take the firm to point B, increasing the output to 20 units.

Figure 5.3	Isoquant map for substitutes and complements

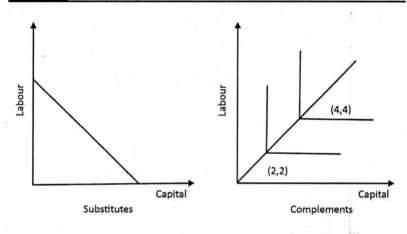

5.5 Returns to Scale

Another important concept in the theory of production is called returns to scale. Returns to scale are defined as the change in the level of output for a proportionate change in the level of input. There are three different types of returns to scale (Figure 5.4): increasing returns to scale, constant returns to scale, and decreasing returns to scale.

Figure 5.4 **Types of returns to scale**

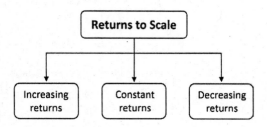

a. **Increasing returns to scale:** Increasing returns to scale is when the percentage change in output is much higher than the percentage change in input. For example, assume that a restaurant owner doubles the number of chefs and the number of kitchens that he owns. If his restaurant can now produce more than double the number of dishes, then it is termed as increasing returns to scale. The pertinent question to ask here is: Why do firms exhibit increasing returns to scale? Do all firms exhibit increasing returns to scale? Increasing returns to scale are exhibited by those firms who have achieved economies of scale. Economies of scale simply means being able to produce a large quantity at a very low cost. This is a result of experience and learning over time. It is a combination of internal economies of scale (resources within the firm), and external economies of scale (shared resources).

b. **Constant returns to scale:** Constant returns to scale occur when the percentage change in output is equal to the percentage change in input. For instance, if the restaurant owner were to double the number of chefs and kitchens, following which the number of dishes produced doubled, it would be a situation of constant returns to scale. Constant returns to scale do not enjoy the advantages of economies of scale. There is no cost advantage in producing at this type of scale.

c. **Decreasing returns to scale:** Decreasing returns to scale occurs when the percentage change in output is less than the percentage change in input. Going by the same example, if the restaurant owner were to double the number of chefs and kitchen, but the number of dishes increased by less than double, it is defined as decreasing returns to scale. Decreasing returns to scale normally occurs due to a lot of internal transaction costs within the firm. This leads to slowing the processes for the firm, leading to lower returns to scale.

It is important to note here that all firms go through different phases of returns to scale from time to time. Most firms start with either decreasing or constant returns to scale and slowly move towards increasing return to scale as the organization becomes larger in size.

5.6 Concluding Remarks

The theory of production is important for firms. It is the building block for the supply curve in the market. The concept of marginal product, and returns to scale have a high degree of applicability in real life. Large multinational organizations today have understood the power of economies of scale, and are therefore positioned in a way to run large businesses in a very cost-effective manner. In addition, firms also have a good understanding of the input mix that is required to produce the highest level of output. We have not touched upon cost, which is the biggest constraint for a firm. The next chapter deals with the cost function of the firm, and talks about how firms decide what to produce, and at what quantity, based on the combination of cost and production facilities.

Quiz

1. **The two major inputs to production are _____ and _____.**

   a. Labor, technology

   b. Technology, capital

   c. Labor, capital

   d. None of the above

2. **The ____ run production function has one factor of production fixed.**

   a. Short

   b. Long

   c. Medium

   d. None of the above

3. **The _____ run production function has _____ factor of production fixed.**

   a. Long; no

   b. Short; one

   c. Long; one

   d. Both a and b

4. **The _____ product of labor _____ over time.**

   a. Total; diminishes

   b. Marginal; diminishes

   c. Marginal; increases

   d. Total; increases

5. **The marginal product is always positive.**

   a. True

   b. False

   c. Cannot be determined

   d. Either a or b

6. **The average product of labor is defined as the total _____ by the total _____.**

   a. Labor; output

   b. Capital; output

   c. Output; labor

   d. Output; capital

7. **If the marginal product of labor increases, the average product of labor will _____.**

   a. Increase

   b. Decrease

   c. First increase then decrease

   d. First decrease then increase

8. When the percentage change in input is _____ than the percentage change in output, it is termed as _____ returns to scale.

    a. Lower; increasing

    b. Lower; decreasing

    c. Higher; increasing

    d. Higher; decreasing

9. When the percentage change in input is _____ than the percentage change in output, it is termed as _____ returns to scale.

    a. Higher; decreasing

    b. Higher; increasing

    c. Lower; constant

    d. Lower; decreasing

10. Marginal product is equal to ___, when total product is at its _____.

    a. One; lowest

    b. Zero; highest

    c. One; highest

    d. Zero; lowest

Answers	1 – c	2 – a	3 – d	4 – b	5 – b
	6 – c	7 – a	8 – a	9 – a	10 – b

Chapter Summary

◆ The production function of the firm is a representation of the inputs that the firm uses to produce a certain level of output.

◆ The production function for a firm is of two types: short-run and long-run.

◆ The short-run production function has one input fixed, with the other input variable. In the long-run production function, both inputs are variable.

◆ The marginal product of an input is the change in output caused by a unit change in input.

◆ The marginal product initially increases and then decreases. It becomes zero at the point when total production is at its maximum. As the total production declines, the marginal product becomes negative.

◆ Isoquants are a representation of the choice of input that the firm uses for the same level of output produced.

◆ The further the isoquant from the origin, the higher the output level.

◆ Returns to scale is defined as the ratio of the percentage change in output to the percentage change in input. It is of three types: increasing, decreasing, and constant.

Chapter 6

Cost

How do firms decide at what price should they sell their products? Pricing decisions are crucial for firms to sustain themselves in the market. The underlying mechanism that allows a firm to decide on the right price is the cost that the firm incurs on producing the good. While there are other factors that affect the pricing decision of the firm (we shall discuss these in later chapters of the book), the cost incurred by the firm is the most important source of information that allows a firm to decide on the pricing strategy. This chapter discusses the different types of cost structures of a firm. It also focuses on the important aspect of economies of scale and how firms can produce more efficiently.

Key learning objectives of this chapter include the reader's understanding of the following:

- The basics of producer theory

- The different types of cost structures a firm faces

- Analyzing the relationship between the different cost structures

- Applying the principles of economies of scale to production decisions

6.1 Introduction

It is important to remember that the final objective of the firm is "profit maximization". [15] Milton Friedman, a famous economist, once mentioned that the business of business is to do business. Hence, firms exist to not only supply goods to society but also to maximize profits for their shareholders. In simple terms, profits are the revenue (R) minus the cost (C). It is mathematically represented as:

$$\Pi = R - C$$

The revenue of the firm is a function of price and quantity. Revenue is equal to the product of the quantity times price. The quantity is a function of the production function, which was discussed in the earlier chapter. In this chapter, we shall focus on the cost side of the firm. Thus, understanding both the production and the cost will enable the firm to maximize profits in the long run.

---

15. Friedman, Milton. "A Friedman Doctrine-- The Social Responsibility of Business Is to Increase Its Profits." The New York Times, September 13, 1970, sec. Archives. https://www.nytimes.com

6.2 Types of Costs

A firm faces two types of cost structures: sfixed cost, and (b) variable cost. The **fixed cost** of a firm is the cost incurred by the firm irrespective of the amount of output produced. Assume a firm, Tom & Jerry, is in the business of selling nutrition bars. The fixed cost would entail the cost of setting up the machines and the cost of buying or renting the land where these nutrition bars would be manufactured. Why is this termed as the fixed cost? It is termed fixed cost because this cost is incurred irrespective of the units of output produced. Whether the firm produces 100 nutrition bars or 1000 nutrition bars, the cost of the machines purchased, and the cost of the factory remain the same. The second type of cost is termed variable cost. The **variable cost** of a firm is the cost that changes with the level of output. Thus, as output begins to increase, the variable cost of the firm increases. Using the same example, if the firm had to employ more people to increase the production of nutrition bars, that would increase the cost of labor. Thus, the total cost of a firm can be split up into the fixed cost and the variable cost. The cost function for a firm is written below:

$$TC(q) = FC + VC(q)$$

The bracketed term denotes that the cost is a function of the output that is being produced. Apart from the fixed cost, the variable and total costs change with changes in the output.

Figure 6.1   **Average cost curves**

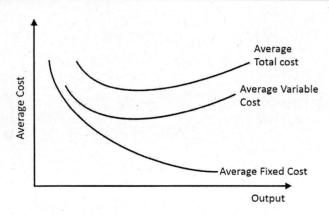

6.2.1 Average and marginal cost

The fixed and variable costs are important concepts for a firm. However, it does not provide much information for the owner or manager to estimate the amount of production required. For example, what should be the optimal amount of nutrition bars that Tom and Jerry should produce? The answer to this lies in asking two specific questions: (a) What is the average cost per unit of nutrition bar (b) What is the additional cost incurred in producing an extra nutrition bar? Both these questions relate to two important concepts in the cost structure, namely, the **average cost** and the **marginal cost**.

Average Total Cost (ATC): The average cost is defined as the cost per unit of goods produced. Thus, if it takes $100 to produce 10 units of nutrition bar, the average cost of a nutrition bar is $10 ($100/10). Mathematically, average cost is defined by:

$$AC = \frac{TC}{q}$$

where, *AC*: average cost; *TC*: total cost; *q*: output produced.

The average cost is a U- shaped curve, which is a combination of the downward-sloping average fixed cost curve, and the upward-sloping average variable cost curve (Figure 6.1).

Average Fixed Cost (AFC): The average fixed cost is defined by the fixed cost divided by the number of units produced. Mathematically, the average fixed cost is defined by:

$$AFC = \frac{FC}{q}$$

The average fixed cost is a downward-sloping curve since the fixed cost is constant irrespective of the number of units produced. Hence, the numerator remains the same, while the denominator increases, causing AFC to decline (Figure 6.1).

Average Variable Cost (AVC): The average variable cost is defined as the variable cost by the number of units produced. Mathematically, the average variable cost is defined as:

$$AVC = \frac{VC}{q}$$

The average variable cost is a U-shaped curve. This is due to the characteristic of diminishing marginal productivity of labor or capital. As the marginal productivity of the input increases initially, and eventually diminishes in the long run, the average variable cost initially declines till a certain quantity and starts to rise thereafter. The shape of the variable cost is inversely related to the shape of the marginal product. When the marginal product increases, the average variable cost declines. When the marginal product decreases, the average variable cost increases.

Marginal Cost: The marginal cost is defined as the additional cost that the firm incurs when an additional unit of output is produced. Thus, if it costs $2 to produce an additional unit of nutrition bar, the marginal cost is $2. Mathematically, the marginal cost is defined as:

$$MC = \frac{\Delta TC}{\Delta q}$$

Where, MC: marginal cost; ΔTC: change in total cost; Δq: and change in quantity.

6.3 Relation Between Marginal Cost and Average Cost: Zones Along the Cost Function

What is the relationship between the marginal cost and the average cost? Look carefully at Figure 6.1. We see that the average cost has a U-shaped curve. This implies that the average cost starts to decrease for the initial level of output that is produced by the firm. It reaches its lowest point, for a particular range of quantity that is produced and starts to increase thereafter. What is the reason behind the U-shaped average cost curve? The U-shaped cost curve is linked to the concept of marginal productivity (discussed in Chapter 5). The marginal productivity increases for the first few units of output that are produced by the firm. It reaches its peak and then starts to diminish soon after. The relation between the marginal product of inputs and the cost curves of the input can be clearly demonstrated in Figure 6.2. As seen, the cost reduces as the marginal productivity increases till point q^*. At q^* the level of production, the marginal productivity is at its highest and the cost is at its lowest. This point is referred to as the point of *minimum efficient scale of production*. It essentially means that at this point, the cost of production of goods is at its lowest.

Figure 6.2   Relationship between marginal productivity and costs

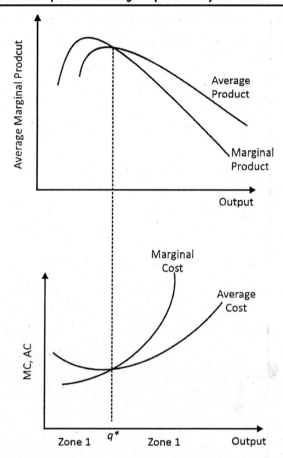

Now, there are two zones in the cost structure for any firm. Zone 1 is when the marginal cost is well below the average cost. Zone 2 is when the marginal cost is well above the average cost. What do these zones imply in real life for firms and organizations? In which zone do firms prefer to be?

Let us understand this through an example. Continuing with the nutrition bar example, assume that the cost to make the first nutrition bar is $2. Thus, the marginal cost is $2. The average total cost is higher, since it also takes into account the average fixed cost. Assume the average total cost is $2. Now, for the second unit, the cost to produce it increases by $1. This is because labor is efficient and hence the marginal cost remains low. From the third unit onwards, the diminishing marginal productivity of labor begins. This implies that by hiring more labor, the output per labor diminishes, which increases the average cost of production. This is when the firm enters Zone 2, wherein the marginal cost of production is higher than the average cost of production. In this zone, the firm is in an inefficient production zone and costs start to increase.

On noticing Figure 6.2, you will see that as marginal cost is less than average cost, average cost falls. As marginal cost is higher than average cost (Zone 2), average cost increases. The intuition behind this is the following: Assume a class of 10 students. If the average GPA of the class is 3.5 out of 4, and if an additional student enters and achieves a GPA of 3.8, then the average GPA of the class is bound to increase. Conversely, if the GPA of the additional student is 3.0 (below the existing class average), then the overall average GPA of the class will fall. Thus, keeping a close eye on the marginal cost for the firm will help the firm analyze which zone it falls under, thereby taking appropriate steps to reduce costs and increase profits.

6.4 The Long-Run Cost Curve

Till this point, we have only spoken about the cost that the firm faces in the short run. The cost curves are the way they are because of certain short-term dynamics. The short-term dynamics are the diminishing marginal productivity of one input. This happens because one factor of production is typically fixed in the short run (recall this from Chapter 5). In this case, the ice cream manufacturer may not have the financial muscle to increase his factories or machinery in the short run. However, it is not true that firms always remain in the short run. What happens then when firms graduate in the long run?

The long-run cost of the firm is an essential concept that provides an implication to understanding how the firm operates from a cost perspective. Figure 6.3 illustrates the long-run cost of the firm. The long-run cost is an envelope of the short-run cost functions of the firm. In simple words, the long-run cost of the firm is the locus of the lowest point of the total short-run cost of the firm. However, just as the short-run, the long-run cost of the firm has a U-shaped curve too. What does this U-shape mean? How is this U-shape different from that of the short-run cost function?

The U-shaped long-run cost function represents the different *economies of scale* for the firm. Economies of scale are defined as the change in cost with respect to the change in output. Simply put, economies of scale are a measure of how the cost for a firm changes when a firm scales up its output. There are two types of economies of scale, namely, economies of scale, and diseconomies of scale. When the firm's long-run cost decreases as the output increases, it is termed as economies of scale. When the firm's long-run cost increases as the output increases, it is termed as diseconomies of scale.

Economies of scale are formally defined as:

$$E_c = \frac{\%\ change\ in\ cost}{\%\ change\ in\ output} = \frac{\frac{\Delta C}{C}}{\frac{\Delta Q}{Q}} = \left(\frac{\Delta C}{\Delta Q}\right)\left(\frac{Q}{C}\right)$$

E_c: Economies of Scale

Note $\left(\frac{\Delta C}{\Delta Q}\right)$ is the marginal cost of the firm. $\left(\frac{Q}{C}\right)$ is the inverse of the average cost of the firm. Hence, the economies of scale can also be defined as:

$$E_c = \frac{MC}{AC}$$

If E_c>1; *MC*>*AC*; the firm incurs diseconomies of scale

If E_c>1; *MC*<*AC*; the firm enjoys economies of scale

If E_c>1; *MC*=*AC*; the firm enjoys constant economies of scale

In other words, by looking at the marginal cost and the average cost, the firm can assess whether it is incurring diseconomies of scale or enjoying economies of scale. When the marginal cost is lower than the average cost, the firm is enjoying economies of scale. When the marginal cost is higher than the average cost, the firm is incurring diseconomies of scale.

Figure 6.3 illustrates this fact. Quantity is measured on the horizontal axis, and cost on the vertical axis. The portion OA represents economies of scale. This is the portion when the long-run cost decreases as the quantity increases. From point A to point B, the long-run average cost remains the same, as the quantity increases (constant returns to scale), while from point B to point C, the cost increases as the output increases (diseconomies of scale).

Figure 6.3 Long-run cost curve for the firm

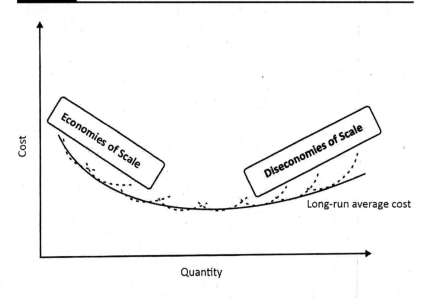

An important point to ponder here is to understand why different firms face different economies of scale. The reasons are numerous. A few of the salient reasons why economies of scale differ across firms are the following:

Scale: The scale (size) of the firm is a big factor that differentiates the economies of scale across firms. Smaller-sized firms face diseconomies of scale due to fixed factors of production. Small firms are unable to expand operations due to a lack of either operational capabilities or the lack of access to finance to expand their operations. Micro, small, and medium enterprises (commonly referred to as MSMEs) typically face this problem. [16] These are small-sized firms that lack the capability to build their products at a large scale. Given that small-sized firms are unable to change all factors of production at the same time, diminishing

---

16. For more reference on MSME's, read the following: World Bank SME Finance: Development news, research, data | World Bank

marginal productivity is higher in smaller firms, which leads to diseconomies of scale. On the other hand, larger firms and multinational corporations have large-scale operations which enable them to lower costs as output increases. This allows them to enjoy economies of scale.

Specialization: Firms that allow specialization of labor enjoy economies of scale. Specialization of labor allows for increased productivity, as labor is now disaggregated based on their core competencies. This resonates with Adam Smith's view of the division of labor. [17] On the other hand, firms that do not practice specialization of labor lead to lower productivity among labor, finally resulting in diseconomies of scale. Firms often cut costs in the short run through labor-sharing practices, however, this leads to a long-run higher cost for the firm.

One important differentiation that should be spelled out is that returns to scale (a concept discussed in Chapter 5), are not the same as economies of scale. Remember, returns to scale deal with the ratio of outputs to inputs. On the other hand, economies of scale deal with the ratio of costs to outputs. It is not necessary that a firm that enjoys increasing returns to scale will also enjoy economies of scale. For instance, a firm may experience increasing returns to scale (where output increases in a greater proportion than inputs), however, if the output produced has a very high cost, the rate of change of cost will be higher than the rate of change of output. This will lead to diseconomies of scale.

---

17. This concept was discussed in the famous book: The Wealth of Nations by Adam Smith

6.5 Concluding Remarks

The cost structure is an important metric for the firm to understand the production size. Apart from that, understanding the cost of each input, and how inputs can be substituted to ensure the lowest possible cost are important implications for the firm's profitability and sustainability in the future. In every industry, there are multiple firms that produce exactly the same goods or services. However, only some of them are profitable, while most others are not. The reason for this difference is that firms that are profitable carefully evaluate their cost structure, so as to provide the output at the lowest possible cost. Therefore, it is imperative that firms closely examine their cost structures and think of alternate ways of reducing costs to produce at the minimum efficient scale of production.

Quiz

1. The _____ cost for a firm is _____ with output levels.

   a. Fixed; constant

   b. Variable; constant

   c. Fixed; variable

   d. Variable; constant

2. The average total cost of a firm follows a _____ shape.

   a. V

   b. U

   c. Linear

   d. Constant

3. The marginal cost curve cuts the average cost curve from below.

   a. True

   b. False

   c. Both a and b

   d. Neither a nor b

4. **Economies of scale are defined when the _____ cost is _____ the _____ cost.**

   a. Marginal; above; average

   b. Average; below; marginal

   c. Marginal, below, average

   d. Average; equal to; marginal

5. **The average cost is at its_____ when the marginal productivity is at its _____.**

   a. Highest; highest

   b. Lowest; lowest

   c. Highest, lowest

   d. Lowest, highest

6. **The average cost follows a U-shaped curve due to _____ productivity of input.**

   a. Increasing marginal

   b. Diminishing average

   c. Diminishing marginal

   d. Increasing average

7. **The minimum efficient scale of production is the point where the average cost of production is at its _____.**

   a. Lowest

   b. Highest

   c. Constant level

   d. None of the above

8. **Average _____ cost is defined as fixed cost by output.**

   a. Variable

   b. Fixed

   c. Total

   d. None of the above

9. **The average fixed cost _____ as output _____.**

   a. Increases; decreases

   b. Decreases; increases

   c. is constant; increases

   d. decreases; is constant

10. The average total cost curve is _____ the average variable cost curve.

    a. Below

    b. Above

    c. To the right of

    d. To the left of

Answers	1 – a	2 – b	3 – a	4 – c	5 – d
	6 – c	7 – a	8 – b	9 – b	10 – b

Chapter Summary

◆ The cost of a firm comprises the fixed cost and the variable cost.

◆ Fixed cost is the cost that the firm incurs irrespective of the level of production. Variable cost is the cost that varies with the level of production.

◆ The average cost of a firm is defined as the overall cost of production per unit. The average cost of a firm follows a U-shaped curve. It declines till a certain level of production and increases thereafter.

◆ The U-shaped average cost of a firm is based on the principle of marginal productivity. In the short run as

◆ The minimum efficient scale of production is the point where the average cost of production is at its lowest.

◆ Economies of scale occur when the long-run cost of the firm decreases as the output increases.

◆ Diseconomies of scale occur when the long-run cost of the firm increases as the output increases.

◆ The long-run cost function is a U-shaped curve, which is the lower envelope of the short-run cost functions.

Chapter **7**

Markets I—Perfect Competition

This chapter is the introduction to a new section of the book, which is going to focus on market structures. It discusses the various kinds of markets. The most important ones are perfect competition, monopoly, and oligopoly. This chapter will focus on the perfect competition market.

Key learning objectives of this chapter include the reader's understanding of the following:

- Understand the distinguishing characteristics of a perfectly competitive market

- Analyze the profit-maximizing output of a perfectly competitive firm

- Evaluate the shut-down and breakeven conditions under a perfectly competitive scenario

- Apply the principles of a perfectly competitive industry in a real-life scenario

7.1 Characteristics of a Perfectly Competitive Market

A perfectly competitive market has four important characteristics. First, there are innumerable buyers and sellers. Second, the goods or products that are sold are homogeneous (there is no product differentiation). Third, there is no bargaining power for either buyers or suppliers. Fourth, there is free entry and exit for firms.

Let us understand this through an example. If you drive through gas stations in a particular county, you will realize that the price of gas is approximately the same across all gas stations. Why is this so? This is because the product (gas) sold is homogeneous and does not differ across sellers. Thus, buyers are indifferent across sellers, and choose the seller that is closest to them. This characteristic makes the price identical across all sellers. Buyers do not have any bargaining power, as the product has many buyers, and no single buyer can influence the price. Similarly, there are many sellers providing the same goods in the market. Hence, no seller has any particular bargaining power in setting the price.

7.2 Price Discovery for a Perfectly Competitive Market

How do firms in a perfectly competitive market set a price? Remember, in such a market, there are innumerable buyers and sellers. Hence, all sellers need to charge the same price to the buyers. What would happen if the price is not the same across all sellers? Obviously, the buyers would navigate to the seller who is charging the lowest price. Imagine that there are 10 ice cream stalls, all selling the same ice cream. The price of an ice cream is $10. One seller reduces the price to $9. All customers start moving to the seller that sells the ice cream for $9. As you would expect, the other sellers will reduce the price to $9, where the new price of the product is now $9. This reduction in price can continue. But for how long? The rule of thumb says that the sellers will reduce the price till the point where the *price is equal to the marginal cost of production*. Any price lower than the marginal cost of production will lead to a loss for the firm. Thus, for a perfectly competitive market, the rule of pricing is Price = Marginal Cost.

Let us understand this through the same example. Assume that a seller sells the ice cream for $10 per unit. The cost of a unit of ice cream is $4. The revenue for the ice cream seller is (price times the quantity). Therefore, if the seller sells one unit, the revenue is $10. If the seller sells 2 units, the revenue is $20. Notice that the total revenue increases at a constant rate as the quantity sold increases. The **average revenue** is defined as the total revenue divided by the total number of units sold. It is formally defined as:

$$Average\ Revenue = \frac{Total\ Revenue}{Quantity\ sold}$$

The **marginal revenue** is defined as the change in total revenue divided by the change in total quantity sold. It is formally defined as:

$$Marginal\ Revenue = \frac{Change\ in\ Total\ Revenue}{Change\ in\ units\ of\ Quantity\ sold}$$

Why is the concept of average and marginal revenue important for the seller? If you go back to Chapter 1, one of the ten principles of economics states that 'people think at the margin'. This implies that when the ice cream seller is selling ice cream, the seller will sell an ice cream only if the marginal revenue is greater than the marginal cost. In this context, if the cost of a unit of ice cream is $4, how many units of ice cream will the seller sell?

Table 7.1 shows the total revenue, average revenue, marginal revenue, and marginal cost for the ice cream seller. Table 7.1 has two important properties. First, the average revenue is always equal to the marginal revenue. This is because as the price is constant ($5), irrespective of the number of units sold, the average and marginal revenue does not change. How does a firm operating in such an industry choose how much to produce? The firm would choose that level of quantity where the marginal revenue is equal to the marginal cost. In this example, the number of units where the marginal unit is equal to the marginal cost of five units. You will notice that at five units, the profit for the firm is the maximum.

Table 7.1		Price, revenue, and profits for a perfectly competitive firm					
Units Sold	Price	Total Revenue	Total Cost	Average Revenue	Marginal Revenue	Marginal Cost	Profits
1	5	5	3	5	5	3	2
2	5	10	5	5	5	2	5
3	5	15	8	5	5	3	7
4	5	20	12	5	5	4	8
5	5	25	17	5	5	5	8
6	5	30	23	5	5	6	7

7.3 Profit Maximization Principle

Firms have a single major objective – to maximize profits. Profits are defined as revenue minus costs. To understand how profit maximization is achieved, look at Figure 7.1 Figure 7.1 illustrates the cost curves that were explained in Chapter 6. The average cost curve has a standard U-shape, while the marginal cost curve first declines and then starts to rise. The marginal cost curve cuts the average cost curve from below. The marginal revenue is equal to the average revenue which is equal to the price. This is a horizontal line as the price is constant irrespective of the amount sold.

| Figure 7.1 | Profit maximizing quantity for a firm in a perfectly competitive industry |

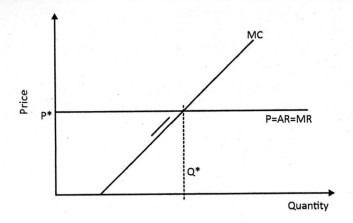

On analyzing Figure 7.1, you would notice that the profit maximization point is q^*, where marginal revenue is equal to marginal cost. This corresponds to five units of output (in the table). But, why is this the case? What would happen if the ice cream seller were to sell either 4 or 6 units of ice cream? If the ice cream seller were to sell four units, the marginal revenue would be higher than the marginal cost, and hence it would be beneficial for the seller to sell one more unit of ice cream. If the ice cream seller sells six units of ice cream, the marginal cost is higher than the marginal revenue. Hence, it would be beneficial if the seller reduces the number of units sold such that marginal cost is reduced. The profit maximization point is, therefore, five units, where the marginal revenue is equal to the marginal cost of production. It is noteworthy to mention that this is also the point where the price is equal to the marginal cost. Hence, the profit maximization rule for a firm operating in a perfectly competitive setting is the point where price is equal to marginal revenue which is equal to the marginal cost.

$$P = MC = MR \qquad (1)$$

If the firm's marginal cost is lower than the marginal revenue, it will *increase* the number of units sold. If the firm's marginal cost is higher than the marginal revenue, it will *decrease* the number of units sold. The profits for the firm are illustrated in the shaded rectangle in Figure 7.1. The profits are the area below the price line and above the average total cost curve.

7.4 Shut-Down Condition

In the previous section, we discussed the profit maximization condition for the firm. However, there could be cases where the firm plans to shut down or exit. This could happen if the firm is facing short-run or long-run costs that exceed the revenue. It is important to understand the difference between shut-down and exit. Shut-down is a temporary (short-run) phenomenon where the firm is unable to recover its variable costs (such as labor costs and electricity), while exit is a permanent (long-run) decision, where the firm is unable to recover both the fixed and variable costs.

The shutdown rule simply states that a firm will shut down if

Total Revenue (pq) < Total Variable Cost(VC)

On dividing both sides of the inequality by quantity (*q*), we get

$$\frac{pq}{q} < \frac{VC}{q}$$

Where VC = variable cost

Variable cost divided by the quantity is the average variable cost (AVC) of production. In other words, when *p<AVC*, the firm will shut down its operations. As long as the price is greater than

the average variable cost, the firm will continue to be in operation. Why is this an important implication for the firm? Remember, in a perfectly competitive industry, the firm is a price taker (the firm has to charge the same price that all other firms are charging in the industry). Hence, only firms that have an average variable cost lower than the price can operate in the market. Remember, when the firm shuts down operations, it still needs to pay the fixed cost (such as rent on machines, and rent for land acquired). These fixed costs are paid by the firm with the optimism that the firm might resume operations soon and may recover them. Shutting down, therefore, is a short-term, temporary phenomenon. The firm will continue to operate if the price is above the variable cost but below the total cost. This is because the firm might be incurring short-term losses (due to high fixed costs), but as long as the firm can cover the variable cost, it can remain in business and be optimistic about a high future demand which will allow it to cover its fixed costs in the long run. The zone from A to B is a zone where the firm is making short-term losses, as the price is below the average total cost.

The supply curve of a firm can be generated from the shut-down condition. Equation (1) states that price should be equal to marginal costs for firms operating within a perfectly competitive industry. The shut-down condition says that this price should be greater than the average variable cost of production. Hence, by combining these two conditions, we get the supply curve of the firm which is the marginal cost of the firm above the average variable costs. Figure 7.2 illustrates this in a better way. The marginal cost curve cuts the average cost curve from below. The supply curve of the firm is the portion of the marginal cost curve that is above the minimum point of the average variable cost (starting from point A upwards). Thus, *the supply curve of the firm is an upward-sloping curve, which is the marginal cost curve above the average cost curve for the firm.*

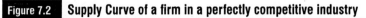

Figure 7.2 Supply Curve of a firm in a perfectly competitive industry

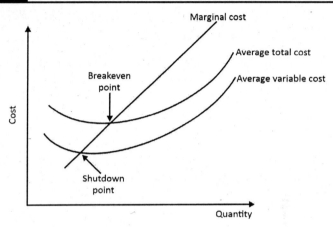

7.5 Exit Conditions for a Firm

In this section, we examine the long-run phenomenon for the firm. A firm will exit the industry only if the total revenue from its operations is unable to cover the total costs. Mathematically, this is represented as:

$$Total\ Revenue < Total\ Cost$$

Dividing both sides of the inequality by quantity (q), we get

$$\frac{pq}{q} < \frac{TC}{q}$$

$$p < ATC$$

Where, ATC = average total cost of production

Thus, an owner of a firm will enter the industry only when the price of goods is greater than the average total cost of production. In other words, the conditions for entry into an industry are:

$$p > ATC$$

What implication does this have for the long-run supply curve of the firm? It implies that the long-run supply curve of the firm is that portion of the marginal cost that is over and above the average total cost. Remember that the average total cost curve is above the average variable cost curve. Hence, the long-run supply curve of the firm begins from a point above the short-run supply curve of the firm.

7.6 Concluding Remarks

The perfectly competitive market is a very popular and common market structure that is prevalent in many economies today. Therefore, it is critical to understand how firms make pricing decisions when they enter such a market. More importantly, it is critical to understand when firms continue their operations as compared to when they should be shutting down operations. For this, a clear understanding of the fixed versus variable cost is important. Many firms today continue their businesses and enter into losses when they are unable to assess the market structure in which they are operating, or unable to completely assess their internal cost structure. Failure to do so leads to outcomes that would not be favorable to the business. Hence, as a firm operating in a perfectly competitive industry, it is important to assess the market structure, the changes in prices, and whether the cost structure of the firm can adhere to the changing prices in order to stay in business.

Quiz

1. A perfectly competitive industry is characterized by _____ buyers and sellers.

    a. Many

    b. Few

    c. No

    d. One

2. In a perfectly competitive market, the bargaining power of buyers is _____.

    a. Zero

    b. One

    c. Infinity

    d. None of the above

3. In a perfectly competitive market, the bargaining power of suppliers is _____

    a. Zero

    b. One

    c. Infinity

    d. None of the above

4. The price that each firm charges in a perfectly competitive industry is _____.

    a. Different

    b. Identical

    c. Zero

    d. One

5. In a perfectly competitive industry, the price is _____ the marginal revenue of the firm.

    a. Equal to

    b. Lower than

    c. Higher than

    d. Not equal to

6. The supply curve of a firm in a perfectly competitive industry is the _____ curve.

    a. Marginal cost

    b. Average variable cost

    c. Average total cost

    d. Fixed cost

7. **The demand curve is _____ for a perfectly competitive firm.**

   a. Vertical

   b. Downward-sloping

   c. Upward-sloping

   d. Horizontal

8. **The shutdown condition for a firm is when the price is _____ the _____ of average variable cost.**

   a. Below; minimum

   b. Above; maximum

   c. Equal to; maximum

   d. Equal to; minimum

9. **The break-even point for a firm in a perfectly competitive industry is when the _____ is _____ the _____.**

   a. Quantity; greater than; marginal cost

   b. Price; equal to; marginal cost

   c. Price; greater than; average total cost

   d. Price; equal to; average total cost

10. Under a perfectly competitive market, the price is always equal to _____.

    a. Average revenue

    b. Marginal revenue

    c. Average cost

    d. Both a and b

Answers	1 – a	2 – a	3 – a	4 – b	5 – a
	6 – a	7 – d	8 – a	9 – d	10 – c

Chapter Summary

◆ A perfectly competitive industry is defined as a market that has many buyers and sellers.

◆ No buyer or seller has any negotiation power over the price. All sellers in the industry are price-takers.

◆ In a perfectly competitive industry, the goods are homogeneous, which means that there is no product differentiation.

◆ The marginal revenue curve for the firm is a horizontal line since the price is constant.

◆ The profit-maximizing condition for a firm is when the price is equal to the marginal cost of the firm.

◆ The shut-down condition for a firm is defined as the point where the price is above the minimum average variable cost of production.

◆ The supply curve for a firm starts from the point where the marginal cost cuts the average variable cost from its minimum point.

CASE STUDY

A Perfectly Competitive Market

Asterix is a firm that sells cage-free eggs in the market. The market is filled with many suppliers and buyers who are interested in consuming eggs. The price of an egg is $5. Asterix sells eggs in the retail market at the price of $5 per egg. The cost of supplying an egg is $2 for Asterix. Hence, Asterix gets a profit of $3 per egg. As this is a perfectly competitive market, with free entry and exit, firms start to notice the profits that can be made in this business and enter the industry. With more firms entering the market, the market share for Asterix drops. This reduces the overall profit for the firm. Hence, in a perfectly competitive market, it is not easy to make supernormal profits.

Discussion Question:

1. What can Asterix do if it needs to gain market share and increase its profits in the long run?

2. Assume that the average variable cost for Asterix is now $6. What decision should Asterix take?

Chapter **8**

Markets II—Monopoly: The Good, Bad, and the Ugly

This chapter discusses the other extreme market form called monopoly. It starts by discussing the main features of a monopolist and then provides the reader with an understanding of the different degrees of monopoly power. The chapter talks about the profit-maximizing condition of a monopolist and discusses the different degrees of price discrimination.

The key learning objectives of this chapter should include the reader's understanding of the following:

- The different features of a monopoly market

- The pricing decision of a monopolist

- Analyzing the degree of monopoly power

- Analyzing the different forms of price discrimination by a monopolist

- Applying the price discrimination method in business and markets

8.1 Introduction

We would have all played the game Monopoly, both as kids and as adults. The game is a replica of what a monopoly is in real life. A monopoly is a market condition where there is only one seller in the market. While this has been the traditional definition of a monopoly, today a monopoly can be defined as a market situation where one player has a large market share in the economy. Is monopoly a good thing? How does a monopoly charge for the good or service it is providing? What can the government do to regulate the monopoly? In this chapter, we are going to discuss these critical issues and provide some real-life examples of how monopolies exist and what governments do to regulate them.

8.2 Monopoly

In the previous chapter, we discussed the market condition called perfect competition. Monopoly lies on the other extreme on a spectrum of market conditions, in terms of the number of sellers. Thus, while perfect competition implies that there are innumerable sellers, **a monopoly is a market condition where there is only one seller.** Given this advantage, the monopolist can charge any price that it wants for the good or service that it is selling. One famous example of a monopoly is the United States Postal Service. For a long period of time, the USPS had the monopoly over delivering letters. Letters were differentiated from documents by weight. Thus, while private courier companies such as FedEx could deliver documents, the delivery of letters rested with the USPS. However, over time, with digitization, the monopoly no longer exists. Today, Facebook (Meta) is considered to be a monopoly in the social media world, Google is a monopoly in the search engine space. How are monopolies created, and more importantly how do they sustain their position? While one might argue that monopolies are created by a first-mover advantage, there is evidence that this is not true. For instance, neither Facebook nor Google were first-movers in their respective spaces. The differentiating aspect is when firms create a sustained competitive advantage [18] over their customers, thereby gaining an exorbitant market share (size), making it difficult for other firms to enter. In other words, unlike perfect competition, the entry and exit barriers in a monopoly market are extremely high. Imagine a firm trying to compete with Facebook in creating an alternate social media platform. It will have to incur a very high fixed cost in setting up the technology, and then waiting for users to use its platform. The switching cost [19] is therefore an important determinant of whether firms can sustain the monopoly. Today, users of Google have a lot of information embedded into Google. Users have email in Gmail, data in Google, and photo memories in Google Photos, which make it difficult for users to shift to

---

18. The term was coined by Michael Porter. For more on this read https://www.hbs.edu/faculty/Pages/item.aspx?num=193

19. Switching cost is the cost incurred by the customer as a result of changing suppliers or brands

any other competitor (if at all they existed). The Economics of Platforms [20] discusses how creating an ecosystem increases the switching cost for consumers, thereby making it difficult for consumers to shift. Similarly, Apple provides the entire ecosystem, from iPhone to Macbook to Airpods thereby creating an ecosystem that makes it difficult for consumers to exit from.

8.3 How do Monopolies Price Their Products?

Pricing decisions are extremely important for a monopolist. Despite having a large market share, it is critical that monopolists charge an optimum price to generate maximum profits. Remember, the objective of the firm is to maximize profits, which is revenue generated minus the costs incurred. However, unlike the market condition of perfect competition, a monopolist does not face a horizontal price (demand) curve. In a perfect competition market, the price of goods remains the same irrespective of the number of units sold. In the case of a monopolist, the price of a good changes depending on how many units are being sold. If the firm sells only one unit, it might charge a very high price, if the firm sells the second unit, it lowers the price, if the firm sells the third unit, the price comes even lower. Why does this happen? Imagine that you are a producer of pencils. Assume that you sell the first unit for $15 (this number should be based on the willingness to pay the consumer). While it is difficult to estimate this number, we assume that a firm extracts the maximum amount of the consumer's willingness to pay. In

---

20. This book was written by Paul Belleflamme and Martin Peitz

other words, the monopolist enjoys a downward-sloping demand curve, with different prices for different units of goods sold. Table 8.1 illustrates the relationship between price and quantity for a monopolist. When the monopolist sells one unit, the price is $10, when he sells two units, the price falls to $9, when he sells three units, the price falls to $8 (Table 8.1). Table 8.1 has one interesting property. The marginal revenue is always lower than the price. For example, when the monopolist is selling the 4th unit from the 3rd unit, the price is $7 each. However, the marginal revenue is only $4. Unlike the perfect competition industry, when the price is always equal to marginal revenue, the monopolist lowers the price for every extra unit that he is able to sell, thereby obtaining a downward-sloping demand curve. *Thus, the demand curve for a monopolist is downward sloping, unlike the horizontal demand curve for a perfectly competitive market.*

Table 8.1   Price, revenue, and profits for a perfectly competitive firm

Quantity	Price	Total Revenue	Average Revenue	Marginal Revenue
0	11	0	-	-
1	10	10	10	10
2	9	18	9	8
3	8	24	8	7
4	7	28	7	4

The monopolist has two effects: (a) price effect, and (b) quantity effect. The price effect is the revenue-reducing effect. As the monopolist increases the quantity it sells, the price declines, and hence revenue decreases. However, the quantity effect is revenue-inducing, as higher sales correspond to higher revenue. Figure 8.1

illustrates the graphical relationship between price and quantity for a monopolist. The average revenue curve, which is the price charged by the monopolist, is the demand curve for the firm. The marginal revenue curve for the firm is, however, lower than the price, and therefore lower than the demand curve.

Figure 8.1   **Profit-maximizing equilibrium for a monopolist**

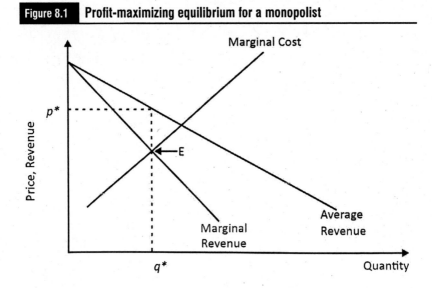

The profit-maximizing point for a firm is when marginal revenue is equal to marginal cost. The marginal cost of a monopolist follows the standard U-shape as discussed in Chapter 6. Point E* is the profit-maximizing point where marginal revenue is equal to marginal cost. Thus, the monopolist produces and sells q* units. What is the price that the monopolist sells it for? Hence, the price charged by the monopolist is p*.

It is easy to see from this figure, what would be the price charged by a firm in a perfectly competitive industry. Remember, the profit-maximizing point for a perfectly competitive firm is also the point where marginal revenue is equal to marginal cost. However, the marginal revenue for a perfectly competitive firm is the price line (demand curve). Hence, , the price that a perfectly competitive firm would charge is p_c at a quantity q_c You will notice that the output of a perfectly competitive firm is higher than the output of a monopolist. Furthermore, the price charged by a firm in a perfectly competitive industry is much lower than that of a monopolist.

8.4 Monopoly Power

How do we assess the power of a monopoly? To what extent are monopolists powerful? It is interesting to know that the power of a monopoly is linked to the elasticity of demand for the product. In other words, the elasticity of demand is inversely related to the power of the monopolist. The degree of monopoly is defined as:

$$L = \frac{P - MC}{P} = -\frac{\%}{E_d}$$

The left-hand side term of the equality $\frac{P-MC}{P}$ describes the markup of price over marginal cost. If the ratio of price over marginal cost is high, then the monopolist is said to have a high power. The monopoly power is inversely related to the elasticity of demand. Why is that so? For goods that have a high degree of elasticity, the consumers do not need to necessarily purchase the product from the monopolist, and hence the degree of monopoly power reduces. Those goods will have many substitutes available, and therefore if the price that the monopolist is charging is very high, the consumer will not buy the product from the monopolist. On the other hand, for goods where the elasticity of demand is very low, the monopoly power increases. This expression is termed **Lerner's Index**. The index has a value of 0 for a perfectly competitive market, as in a perfectly competitive market (P = MC), and hence the numerator is equal to zero.

8.5 Social Cost of a Monopoly

The monopolist charges a price where marginal revenue is equal to marginal cost. However, unlike a perfectly competitive market, the marginal revenue is not equal to the demand curve. The willingness to pay (value attached) by the buyer is given by the demand curve. The cost for the monopolist is given by the cost curve. In equilibrium, the demand curve should intersect the cost curve to produce socially efficient output. This happens in the case of a firm operating in a perfectly competitive market, where the profit point is when the demand curve is equal to the marginal cost curve. However, under a monopoly, the profit-maximizing output is lower than the socially efficient output, causing a deadweight loss. A deadweight loss is a loss in overall social welfare for the economy as that part of output is not produced, and hence neither producers gain, nor consumers. Figure 8.2 shows the socially efficient output q_c. However, the monopoly output is much lower. The gap between these outputs is the deadweight loss to society. That portion of output is lost, as monopolists do not produce it (and hence do not gain profits), and consumers do not consume it. It is tempting to think that all monopoly markets cause a decline in overall social welfare. While this is true for most monopoly markets, there can be cases where the monopolist serves the needs of the entire market through price discrimination. We shall study this in detail in the next section.

| Figure 8.2 | **Social welfare cost of a monopolist** |

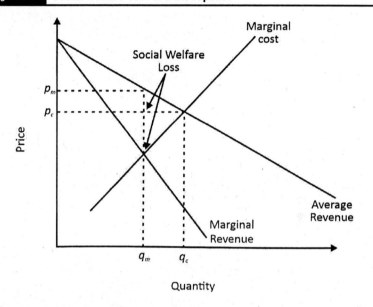

8.6 Price Discrimination

Till this point, we have assumed that the monopolist is charging the same price to all its customers. Thus, when the monopolist reduces the price to sell an extra unit of the good, the price is reduced for all consumers. This, however, may not always be the case. Monopolists have the power to discriminate among consumers and charge a price that is not uniform among consumers. This practice of charging different sets of prices to different sets of consumers is known as **price discrimination**. Price discrimination requires three conditions. First, consumers should be able to be separated either geographically or by their willingness to pay. Second, price discrimination cannot take place in a competitive market. Third, there should be little or no scope for arbitrage to occur.

Price discrimination is of three kinds as described below:

First degree: First-degree price discrimination occurs when the monopolist extracts the entire surplus from the consumers. Consumer surplus is defined as the difference between the willingness to pay by the consumer, and the price that the consumer is actually paying. For instance, if you were willing to pay $5 for a can of Diet Coke, but the market price is $3, then the consumer surplus is $2 ($5 - $3). In other words, the consumer surplus is the area below the demand curve, and above the price line. However, for the first can of Coke, the consumer is willing to pay $5 (from the demand curve). Similarly, for the second can of Coke, the price that the consumer pays remains $3, however, the willingness to pay is $4. Hence, the area above the price line and below the demand curve is the entire consumer surplus.

In first-degree price discrimination, the monopolist charges different consumers different prices, such that the monopolist extracts the entire surplus from the consumer. In this case, the monopolist charges different prices to different sets of consumers, thereby extracting the entire consumer surplus from the market. A good example of first-degree price discrimination is surge pricing by cab aggregators like Uber. When consumers are in a hurry or are desperately looking for a cab, Uber charges a premium that is very specific to an individual. The price charged to one individual may not be the same for the other. This type of price discrimination is termed first-degree price discrimination.

Example 8.1: Airline Pricing (Application of first-degree price discrimination)

Most airlines practice dynamic pricing. This implies that prices fluctuate depending on the current demand. For instance, if there is a holiday season coming close, or a demand or tourism, then prices will start to rise. On the contrary, if demand is low, the tickets sell for a very low price to boost demand. All flyers sitting on the same plane do not pay the same price. Flyers that book their tickets well in advance get a lower price for their ticket as compared to someone who is looking for a last-minute travel. In this way, airlines try to capture the consumer surplus from each customer, charging different prices to different customers. This form of price discrimination increases the firm's profits by taking advantage of some consumer's higher willingness to pay.

Second degree: Second-degree price discrimination is also known as block pricing. This kind of price discrimination occurs when the monopolist charges different prices based on the quantity purchased. Second-degree pricediscrimination is the easiest form of price discrimination for the monopolist as it does not require much effort to segment customers. Second-degree price discrimination is very popular across retail markets. When retailers provide bulk discounts, such as buy 2 get 1 free, or buy goods worth $500 and get a 10 % discount, these are examples of second-degree price discrimination.

Why is second-degree price discrimination a popular form of pricing? First, this form of price discrimination allows sellers to sell higher quantities to buyers. Given that sellers achieve economies of scale while producing more, selling a higher quantity helps them achieve higher revenues. Second, it helps sellers utilize inventory more efficiently. A popular problem for many retailers is unused inventory. This form of price discrimination helps utilize inventory in an efficient and profitable manner.

Second-degree price discrimination is also useful when governments want consumers to use less of a good. Consider the consumption of electricity. When governments want consumers to use less electricity in order to achieve greater sustainability of resources, they can practice second-degree price discrimination on pricing electricity. In many countries, consumers are charged a different price per unit of electricity, depending on the total amount of electricity consumed in that billing cycle. For instance, if a household has consumed fewer units than a particular benchmark of consumption, the household enjoys a lower price per unit. On the contrary, if the household has exceeded the consumption units above a particular threshold level, the household would no longer enjoy the lower price. Therefore, by placing levels (bands) on the electricity consumption levels, and charging different prices for different bands, governments practice second-degree price discrimination, ensuring that energy consumption is at a sustainable level.

Example 8.2: Software and Telecom (Application of second-degree price discrimination)

Most telecom and software enterprises practice second-degree price discrimination. This form of discrimination implies pricing the good based on the quantity purchased by the consumer. For instance, many telecom companies price their data packs and call charges at a lower rate if the consumer takes an annual pack as compared to a monthly pack. Similarly, software enterprises like Adobe have different pricing packages for individuals who take the subscription for a longer period of time.

Third degree: Third-degree price discrimination occurs when the monopolist charges different prices in different markets. Consider a monopolist selling its products across two or more different geographies. The monopolist can charge different prices in different markets. How is this price determined? Generally speaking, the price is determined based on the elasticity of demand in both markets. Markets with a higher elasticity of demand are generally charged a lower price, while the market with a lower elasticity of demand is charged a higher price. Why does this happen? Markets characterized by a high elasticity of demand will be more affected by a price increase, compared to markets characterized by a low elasticity of demand. Consumers who have a high elasticity of demand will find alternatives and substitutes for the product if the monopolist were to charge a very high price. On the contrary, consumers with a low elasticity of demand would buy the goods irrespective of the price increase by the monopolist. Hence, the rule of thumb is higher the price elasticity of demand, the lower the price in that market, and the lower the price elasticity of demand, the higher the price in that market.

Third-degree price discrimination is a very common form of price discrimination by many businesses. Consider airlines that charge a higher price for people booking their tickets closer to the travel date than for those who plan their travel well in advance. Airlines know that consumers looking for tickets closer to the travel date have a well-defined inelastic demand (probably due to some urgency), and hence charge a much higher price than what another consumer would have paid for the same route months ago. This is a case of third-degree price discrimination.

Example 8.3: Restaurant Pricing (Application of third-degree price discrimination)

Most restaurants and fast-food service joints have differentiated pricing for students and other set of customers. The price for a student or (a kid-meal) is priced lower due to the lower purchasing power. Since the restaurant wants to boost the demand from these set of consumers, they offer a lower and differentiated set of prices. This is a case of third-degree price discrimination where the price is charged based on the elasticity of demand in different markets. Since students are price sensitive, the price charged for them is lower as compared to adults who are not as price-sensitive as students. The rule of thumb is to charge a lower price for customers in the market that has a high price elasticity of demand and charge a higher price for customers in the market that has a low-price elasticity of demand.

8.7 Conclusion

So, are monopolies good or bad or ugly? While Figure 8.2 shows that there is a deadweight loss to society and a loss to economic welfare in the case of a monopoly, this might not always be true. A monopolist can also increase social welfare by reducing exclusion. Consider the case of price discrimination, where the monopolist charges different prices to different sets of customers. If the monopolist were to charge a single price, then those consumers who possibly benefit from a lower price due to the practice of price discrimination would have been excluded from receiving the goods. Governments can regulate monopolies to improve social welfare. First, the government can have strict regulations around the functioning of a monopoly and keep a price check on the monopolist. The government can reduce the monopoly power by providing the good itself. For example, the United States Postal Service and other utility companies in the United Kingdom and in other parts of the globe are examples of the governments running the business solely. This is often termed a natural monopoly. Lastly, the government should open up the market by fostering efficient competition that can reduce social welfare loss.

Quiz

1. **A monopoly market is defined as a market where there is only ____ seller.**

   a. One

   b. Two

   c. Few

   d. None of the above

2. **The degree of monopoly power depends on the difference between price and ____.**

   a. Marginal cost

   b. Average cost

   c. Variable cost

   d. Fixed cost

3. **The value of the Lerner's Index in a perfectly competitive firm is ____.**

   a. Infinite

   b. One

   c. Zero

   d. None of the above

4. _____ degree price discrimination is a practice where the monopolist charges a price based on the quantity purchased by the consumer.

   a. First

   b. Second

   c. Third

   d. None of the above

5. _____ degree price discrimination is a practice where the monopolist charges different price points for different market segments.

   a. Second

   b. First

   c. Third

   d. None of the above

6. Deadweight loss is the loss due to the difference in _____ between a perfectly competitive market and a monopolist market.

   a. Output

   b. Price

   c. Cost

   d. Profit

7. First-degree price discrimination is the practice of the monopolist to extract the entire ____- surplus.

   a. Producer

   b. Government

   c. Consumer

   d. None of the above

8. If United Parcel Services charges a different price to consumers on the East Coast as compared to the West Coast, it is termed as _____ degree price discrimination.

   a. First

   b. Second

   c. Third

   d. Zero

9. When a firm charges a different price to different consumers based on the willingness to pay, it is called _____ degree price discrimination.

   a. Second

   b. Third

   c. First

   d. Zero

10. A monopolist faces a _____ sloping demand curve.

    a. Horizontally

    b. Vertically

    c. Downward

    d. Upward

Answers	1 – a	2 – a	3 – c	4 – b	5 – c
	6 – a	7 – c	8 – c	9 – c	10 – c

Chapter Summary

◆ Monopoly is defined as a market structure where there is only one seller.

◆ The demand curve for a monopolist is downward-sloping.

◆ The monopoly power is a function of the elasticity of demand in the market.

◆ Lerner's Index is a measure of monopoly power, which is the ratio of price minus marginal cost over price.

◆ Price discrimination is the practice of charging different sets of prices to different customers.

◆ There are three degrees of price discrimination: first-degree, second-degree, and third-degree.

- 1st degree price discrimination is the practice of charging different prices to different consumers.

- 2nd degree price discrimination is the practice of charging different prices based on the consumption bundle.

- 3rd degree price discrimination is the practice of charging different prices based on segmentation.

Chapter 9

Markets III—Game Theory and Oligopolistic Markets

In the previous two chapters, we focused on the two extreme forms of markets, namely, perfectly competitive markets, and monopoly. In this chapter, we are going to focus on a more popular and practical market structure that lies between these extremes. It is termed an oligopoly. While a perfectly competitive market has many sellers, and a monopoly has only one seller, an oligopolistic market has very few sellers, with each seller having significant market power. Consequently, the market actions of one firm have an effect on other firms. Therefore, unlike perfect competition, firms in an oligopolistic market are interdependent. The nature of an oligopolistic market provides an opportunity to apply game theory in microeconomics. Game theory helps to understand the behavior of firms in oligopolistic markets. In a monopoly market, since there is only one player, there is no strategic interaction among firms. Similarly, in a perfectly competitive market, there are multiple firms providing the same goods. Hence, there is no scope for any strategic interaction. In an oligopolistic firm, however, market power is enjoyed by a few firms selling slightly different varieties of the same good. Most firms operating in the market are oligopolistic in nature. Hence, understanding game theory and its applications to such firms becomes indispensable.

The key learning objectives of this chapter include the reader's understanding of the following

- The characteristics of an oligopolistic market structure

- Applying the principles of game theory to strategic decision-making

- Understanding the concept of Nash Equilibrium and how this equilibrium is reached

- Assessing the difference between different types of games including simultaneous and sequential games

9.1 Game Theory and Oligopoly Markets

Game theory as a discipline was introduced by the famous economist John Nash. Game Theory has applications in various fields including warplay, medicine, firm behavior, government policy, and international economic affairs. Game theory deals with strategic thinking and strategic decision-making among different entities, including individuals, firms, and countries. In the language of game theory, the people playing the game are often referred to as players. Game theory has a big application in understanding oligopolistic markets.

Let us understand the simplest form of an oligopoly which is a duopoly. A duopoly is a market structure with only two firms in the market. Assume there are two firms (A and B) operating in the market, selling two products each. The market demand for the product is shown in Table 9.1. We assume, for simplicity, that the marginal cost of production is zero. As the quantity produced and sold increases, the price decreases. The price and the total revenue are shown in Table 9.1. Now, if this was a perfectly competitive market, the price would be equal to the marginal cost of the firms. On the other hand, if this was a monopoly, the price would be equal to $60, selling 60 units at a revenue of 3600. How would the duopoly market react in this scenario? Who would produce how much? One way to think of this is that the two firms within the duopoly market collude and form a cartel. A cartel is a group that is formed by organizations with a common goal in mind. In a cartel, firms often collude. Collusion is the act of an agreement among firms in a cartel, either towards charging a particular price or producing a particular quantity. For instance, in this example, both firms can form a cartel and collude to produce 30 units each, with the total market production being 60 units. The price is $60, and the total revenue that each firm gains is $1,800. However, it is critical to note here that each firm in the duopoly market has an incentive not to cooperate with each other, with the aim of increasing their own profits. This action of defaulting can cause short-term gains for each firm.

Consider the case where one firm increases its production from 30 units to 40 units. The other firm continues to produce 30 units. The total amount of production is, therefore, 70 units. At this production, the price is $50. Hence, the firm producing 40 units, gets a revenue of $2,000, while the firm producing 30 units gets a revenue of $1,500. You will be beginning to notice that there is an incentive in defaulting from the original collusion regarding the same price. However, it would be foolish to imagine that the other firm does not think the same way too. If the second firm now acts similarly and produces 40 units, the total production increases to 80 units. The resulting price falls to $40. With both firms producing 40 units each, the revenue is now $1,600 for each firm. Notice how the total revenue for each firm has fallen from $1,800 (in collusion) to $1,600 (after defaulting). Thus, it is beneficial for both firms to collude.

This equilibrium is termed as nash equilibrium. A Nash equilibrium is a state of equilibrium wherein the strategy of each of the players is the best response given the other person's strategy such that there is no gain by altering the individual strategy. In simple words, a Nash equilibrium is a state of equilibrium in which the player will continue to choose the current strategy given the strategy chosen by the other player, having no incentive to deviate from it.

| Table 9.1 | Output, price, and revenue table |

Output	Price	Total Revenue (Profit)
0	120	0
10	110	1100
20	100	2000
30	90	2700
40	80	3200
50	70	3500
60	60	3600
70	50	3500
80	40	3200
90	30	2700

9.2 How Cooperation Works

A very famous example and analogy of cooperation using game theory principles is known as the **Prisoner's Dilemma**. The prisoner's dilemma is very interesting as it explains the applications of strategic thinking, cooperation, and competition (Table 9.2). The game is as follows. There are two suspects who are caught for committing a crime. The police interrogate them separately in different rooms. Each prisoner has the option to either confess or deny. The punishment given by the police officer is the following. If one prisoner confesses, and the other remains silent, then the prisoner who confesses gets no punishment (zero years of imprisonment), while the prisoner who remains silent gets a punishment (five years of imprisonment). If both confess, both get moderate punishment (three years each). If both stay silent, both get one year of imprisonment.

Now, the best outcome for the prisoners will be for both of them to remain silent. However, each prisoner might feel that the other prisoner will confess, and hence they will face the risk of getting a punishment of a higher degree. The dominant strategy, then, for each prisoner is to confess. A **dominant strategy** is a strategy that one player chooses irrespective of the strategy adopted by the other player. In this case, if Prisoner 1 confesses, Prisoner 2 should also confess, since he will get three years of imprisonment compared to five years if he denies it. Similarly, if Prisoner 1 denies, and Prisoner 2 confesses, Prisoner 2 will get zero years of imprisonment, compared to one year if he denies. Hence, the dominant strategy for Prisoner 1 is to confess. Using the same logic, the dominant strategy for Prisoner 2 is also to confess. Therefore, both prisoners finally confess. Both prisoners confessing is, therefore, the **Nash Equilibrium** of the game. The outcomes of a game are defined as payoffs. Hence, the numbers in brackets are payoffs for each player.

Table 9.2 Prisoners' dilemma

Prisoner Strategy	Prisoner 2 Confesses	Prisoner 2 Denies
Prisoner 1 Confesses	(3,3)	(0, 5)
Prisoner 1 Denies	(5, 0)	(1,1)

The prisoner's dilemma has applications to various other disciplines such as economics, business, and politics. Consider two firms, say Coca-Cola and Pepsi, selling similar products (Table 9.3). Each must decide on a pricing strategy. They exploit their joint market power the best when both charge a high price; each makes a profit of ten million dollars per month. If one sets a competitive low price, it pulls a lot of customers away from the rival, and gets a profit of $15 million, while the other firm gets $0. If both set low prices, the profits of each decline to $5 million each. Here, the low-price strategy is akin to the prisoner's confession, and the high-price is akin to keeping silent. The former strategy of reducing the price is then the dominant strategy for each firm. It is obvious that both firms can be better off by charging a high price together. However, the inability to be able to maintain the position leads to firms making sub-optimal decisions.

What are the possible policy options to allow for better cooperation among players? A few of the options that would lead to higher cooperation among players are the following. First, if the game is being played only for one time or for a fixed period of time, then achieving cooperation is difficult. However, if the game is a long-term one, then achieving cooperation is easier. For example, if both firms knew that they would be in the industry for a very long period of time, it would be better to cooperate in their actions. Second, if the decisions (actions) are public, and not private, then cooperation is better than defecting. In this case, changing the price of the product is a very visible decision that will be observed by other firms in the market. Hence, it is better that the firm complies with the price collusion and does not deviate.

Table 9.3   Price-determining strategies for firms

Company Strategy	Maintain price	Reduce price
Maintain price	(10, 10)	(0, 15)
Reduce price	(15, 0)	(5,5)

9.3 Simultaneous Versus Sequential Games

Strategic interactions between economic actors in an environment can be of two forms, namely, simultaneous or sequential. A **simultaneous game** is one where all participants make their decision at the same time. A **sequential game** is one where participants make their decisions in a particular sequence. These decisions could be about the amount of output to produce or the price to charge. A sequential game is when the market has a *leader* and a *follower*. The leader carefully observes the follower and then makes a decision that allows it to maximize its objectives.

Take the same example of Coke and Pepsi in the carbonated beverage market. The game can be turned into a sequential game as seen in Figure 9.1. Coke is trying to decide whether to develop a new product variety, Coke Green. The payoff situation (in profits) is the following: if Coke develops the product, it will get $600 million if Pepsi develops a new product too, and $800 million if Pepsi chooses not to develop a new product. If Coke doesn't develop a new product, it will get $200 million if Pepsi develops a new product, and $400 million if Pepsi doesn't. If Coke does develop a new product, then Pepsi will get $600 million if it develops one too, and only $200 million if it doesn't develop one. If Coke does not develop a new product, then Pepsi will get $800 million if it also comes out with a new product, and only $400 million if it doesn't launch one. Figure 9.1 shows the **decision tree** framework. The first number is the bracketed term is the profit for the first mover (Coke), and the second number is for Pepsi.

Figure 9.1	**Sequential move game**

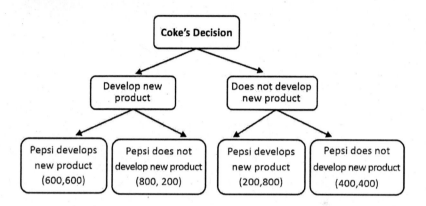

This game is solved through a process known as **backward induction**. Backward induction is a traditional way to solve a sequential game, where one player goes first, and the other follows later. In this case, Coke makes the decision first whether or not to develop a product. In backward induction, the player going first solves the game backward. In other words, it sees what the end result is and then takes the appropriate steps. In this scenario, Coke knows that if it develops the product, then Pepsi will definitely develop the product. This is because Pepsi will gain a profit of $600 million by developing the product, versus $200 million if it does not. Thus, both firms will get a profit of $600 million. Similarly, if Coke does not develop the product, Pepsi will definitely develop the product, as the profit for Pepsi to develop the product is more ($800 million) versus not developing ($400 million). Thus, in either case, Pepsi will develop the product. Thus, developing a new product is the **dominant strategy** for Pepsi. Given this, Coke will now think of the game as the following: If Pepsi is anyway going to develop the product, it is in its best interest to develop the product too. By developing the product, I get a profit of $600 million versus $200 million if I do not develop a product. Hence, in the end, both Coke and Pepsi develop new products in the market. This is the Nash equilibrium for the game.

9.4 Cheap Talk and Empty Threats

It is often seen in businesses that firms signal an action to other firms. The method of signaling implies that the firm chooses an action that tells the other firm that it is going to employ a strategy in the near future, in the hope that the other firm gets the signal and acts appropriately. However, not all signals are credible threats. Consider an example where Coke signals to Pepsi that it is launching a new product variety. It does so by opening up a new factory and making a public announcement that it has discovered the concentrate for a new variety. This is a case of a credible threat, as setting up a new factory and investing in research and development comes at a cost. Thus, Pepsi should consider this as a credible signal and act appropriately. On the contrary, if Coke does not provide any signal of a credible threat, then Pepsi may feel that Coke is not going to launch a new product and will choose its decisions appropriately.

Consider the scenario depicted in Figure 9.1. If Pepsi wants Coke to take its signal as a credible threat, such that it can enjoy a higher payoff in the longer run, it should provide a credible signal such as a public announcement of a new concentrate or the opening of a new factory. In this case, Pepsi will develop a new product too and both will enjoy a higher profit of $600 million each, compared to the case where Pepsi feels that Coke will not launch a new variety.

9.5 First-Mover Advantage

A first-mover advantage is an advantage that is gained by a firm by entering the market first. The advantages could be in the form of economies of scale, lesser competition, and greater market share. It also has the advantage of setting the price and quality benchmark. How does the first-mover advantage really work? Consider the same game of Coke versus Pepsi as shown in Figure 9.1. In this game, Coke is moving first, and Pepsi follows. Coke knows that if it develops a new product, then Pepsi will follow suit as Pepsi will gain a profit of $600 million versus $200 million if Pepsi does not develop a new product. Similarly, if Coke does not develop a new product, Pepsi will still develop a new product, as the profit for Pepsi will be $800 million, versus $400 million if it does not. Therefore, Coke now knows that Pepsi will definitely develop a new product. Coke now has to compare between just two options as compared to four. Given that Pepsi will develop a new product, Coke knows that it will receive a higher profit if it develops a new product too ($600 million), as compared to $200 if it does not. Hence, the end result is that both firms end up developing new products and get a profit of $600 million each.

Now, let us flip the story. Assume that Pepsi enters the market first and is the first mover. Pepsi has two options. It can develop a new product or not. If Pepsi develops a new product, and Coke develops a new product, the profits are $600 each. If Pepsi develops a new product, while Coke does not, the profits are $800 for Pepsi and $200 for Coke. If Pepsi does not develop a new product, while Coke develops, the profits are $200 million for Pepsi and $800 million for Coke. Lastly, if neither Pepsi nor Coke develops new products, the profits are $400 million for each. If Pepsi is the first mover, Pepsi knows that if it develops a new product, then Coke will follow suit as Coke will gain a profit of $600 million versus $200 million, if Pepsi does not develop a new product. Similarly, if Pepsi does not develop a new product, Coke will still develop a new product, as the profit for Coke will be $800 million, versus $400 million if it does not. Therefore, Pepsi now knows that Coke will definitely develop a new product. Pepsi now has to compare between just two options as compared to four. Given that Coke will develop a new product, Pepsi knows that it will receive a higher profit if it develops a new product too ($600 million), as compared to $200 if it does not. Hence, the end result is that both firms end up developing new products and get a profit of $600 million each. You will notice that there is no specific advantage here for anyone moving first. The final profit for each firm remains the same. However, if the payoffs were to change, there could be a case for a first-mover advantage. Consider Figure 9.2. The game remains the same, however, the profits under each condition are different.

Figure 9.2 **Sequential game with Coke as the leader**

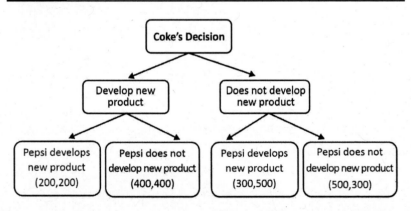

Consider the case where Coke is the first mover. Coke knows that if it develops a new product, Pepsi will not develop as

Pepsi gains a profit of $400 million by not developing versus $200 million by developing. On the other hand, if Coke does not develop a new product, Pepsi will develop a new product as the profit Pepsi gets in this case is $500, versus $300 if it does not develop. Hence, the decision for Pepsi to develop depends on Coke. Knowing this, Coke will develop as the profit Coke gets if it develops is $400, versus $300 if it does not develop. The Nash equilibrium is (400, 400), where Coke develops and Pepsi does not.

Consider Figure 9.3, where Pepsi is now the leader. On flipping the story, and making Pepsi the leader, we see that Coke will decide not to develop the product if Pepsi develops the product. This will give Coke a profit of $300 million compared to $200 million if they develop the product. On the other hand, Coke will not develop the product, if Pepsi does not develop the product. This will give Coke a profit of $500 million, compared to $400 million if it develops the product. Now Pepsi knows that Coke will not develop the product. The decision that will give Pepsi the highest profit is if it develops the product, and gets a profit of $500 million. Thus, the Nash Equilibrium is (500, 300), with Pepsi developing the product, and Coke not developing the new product. Compare this outcome to the previous outcome when Coke was the leader. When Coke was the leader, the profit of Coke was $400, which has been reduced to $300. On the other hand, when Pepsi is the leader, the profit is $500, compared to the previous case of $400. Hence, in this scenario, having the first move is advantageous.

| Figure 9.3 | Sequential game with Pepsi as the leader |

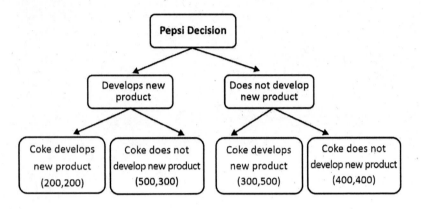

9.6 Conclusion

Oligopolistic markets are the most popular type of market structures that are present today. With competition arising among firms across all sectors, the practical application of game theory in firm-level decision-making becomes very prominent. Competitive decision-making could be at the price level, quantity level, or critical decision variables, such as entry into a new geographical area or the launching of a new product variety. Understanding the basic framework of game theory in decision-making helps in analyzing competitors' decisions. While game theory is a subject by itself, this chapter reviews the important preliminary concepts that are applicable to oligopolistic markets.

Quiz

1. **An oligopoly is a market structure where there are _____ sellers with _____ market power.**

   a. Many, small

   b. Few, large

   c. Few, small

   d. Many, large

2. **A _____ strategy is one which the firm chooses irrespective of what the other firm chooses.**

   a. Dormant

   b. Dominant

   c. Complement

   d. Supplement

3. **A _____ game is one where one player moves first, followed by the other.**

   a. Simultaneous

   b. Sequential

   c. Nash

   d. Coordinated

4. _____ induction is the method by which the leader looks at the final probable solution of the game and chooses its strategy.

   a. Forward

   b. Coordinated

   c. Backward

   d. Linked

5. A _____ is a market structure with _____ two firms.

   a. Duopoly; Only

   b. Monopoly; More than

   c. Oligopoly; Less than

   d. None of the above

6. First-mover advantage can be achieved due to:

   a. Economies of scale

   b. Greater access to market share

   c. Both a and b

   d. Neither a nor b

7. A _____ game is where both players play together.

   a. Sequential

   b. Simultaneous

   c. Forward

   d. Backward

8. **Solving the game from the last stage to the first is called _____.**

   a. Backward induction

   b. Forward induction

   c. Backward integration

   d. Forward integration

9. **A _____ strategy is one which a player chooses irrespective of what the other players choose.**

   a. Dominant

   b. Weak

   c. Subordinate

   d. None of the above

10. **A _____ threat is when a firm/actor makes a decision to signal to the other firm.**

   a. Empty

   b. Credible

   c. Good

   d. Bad

Answers	1 – b	2 – b	3 – b	4 – c	5 – a
	6 – c	7 – b	8 – a	9 – a	10 – b

Chapter Summary

◆ An oligopoly is characterized by one with few sellers having significant market power.

◆ Firms in an oligopolistic market need to take strategic decisions and actions that will help them fight market competition.

◆ Game Theory is the study of decision-making among firms, individuals, or different entities.

◆ Nash equilibrium is an equilibrium wherein the strategy of each of the players is the best response, given the other person's strategy and no participant can gain by changing his/her own strategy.

◆ The dominant strategy for a player is the strategy that the player will choose irrespective of the decision chosen by the other player.

◆ Games can be of two types: simultaneous and sequential. Simultaneous games are those where both actors decide and take action together. Sequential games are those where there is a leader and a follower.

◆ First-mover advantage can be profitable depending on the payoffs that the players receive.

Chapter **10**

Macroeconomics: It's the Economy, Stupid

How does an economy function? How does one assess whether an economy is growing? You have probably heard names like GDP, inflation, and unemployment in the media and news articles. This chapter is an introduction to the macroeconomic environment. It discusses the role of various factors in the functioning of the overall economy. The chapter specifically focuses on the building blocks of the economy, by discussing in detail the five different sectors that constitute the economy. Lastly, the chapter ends by comparing the different ways in which the national income of an economy is measured. After understanding the importance of macroeconomic variables, one can join the dots to understand the linkages between them and how each variable affects the economy's growth.

Key learning objectives of this chapter include the reader's understanding of the following:

- Assessing the building blocks of an economy

- Analyzing how the circular flow of income plays an integral role in economic growth

- Understanding how the gross domestic product of an economy is computed

- Evaluating the different variations of gross domestic product

10.1 The Circular Economy

10.1.1 The two-sector economy

The starting point to studying an economy's growth is understanding the circular flow of income. The circular flow of income starts from a simple two-sector model. The two sectors are households and firms. Households provide labor to firms and firms provide goods and services to households. Firms use this labor to produce goods and services. In exchange, firms provide goods and services to consumers and individuals in households for a particular price. The revenue that firms earn by selling these goods and services is then invested back into the enterprise to sustain the business. Figure 10.1 represents the two-sector model. The circular flow works in two stages. In the first stage, households provide labor (factors of production) to firms. Firms provide wages (factor incomes) to households in return for their labor. In the second stage, firms use this labor to produce goods and services which are sold to households, and households purchase them at a price that is paid to firms as consumption expenditure.

| Figure 10.1 | The two-sector economy |

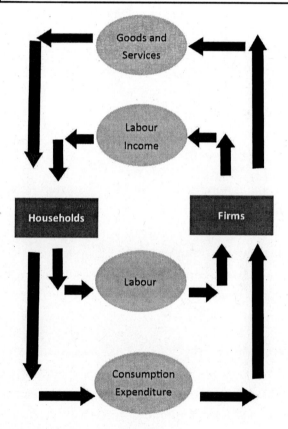

10.1.2 The three-sector economy

The three-sector model includes the government in the circular flow of income. The role of the government is to collect taxes from households and corporations. The households pay taxes to the government in the form of income tax, while the corporations pay taxes to the government in the form of corporate tax. Using these taxes, the government provides state infrastructure services such as roads, railways, ports, and telecommunication services to the individuals and enterprises in the economy. Thus, the government receives revenue in the form of household income taxes and corporate taxes, and incurs expenditures towards infrastructure activities, and social welfare programs.

The government and the firms: The governments receive corporate taxes from firms that produce goods and services. Additionally, it also provides subsidies to firms that are working in certain sectors. For instance, governments in developing economies provide subsidies to firms working in the clean energy sector.

The government and the households: the government collects taxes in the form of income taxes. It then provides services to the households by building infrastructure such as railways, ports, roads, and telecommunication services. In addition, it also provides social welfare programs in many developing economies, and transfer payments such as old-age pension schemes as well as expenditure towards the salaries for government professionals.

The government and the households: the government collects taxes in the form of income taxes. It then provides services to the households by building infrastructure such as railways, ports, roads, and telecommunication services. In addition, it also provides social welfare programs in many developing economies, and transfer payments such as old-age pension schemes as well as expenditure towards the salaries for government professionals.

The government maintains a budget which is a list of the revenue and the expenditure items. If the revenue exceeds the expenditure, the budget is said to be in surplus. If the expenditure exceeds the revenue, it is said to be in deficit.

Figure 10.2 represents the three-sector model. It builds upon the two-sector model. However, the government is added as another entity. As shown in the Figure, the role of the government is to collect taxes from households and firms and provide subsidies and infrastructure to firms and households.

Figure 10.2 **The three-sector economy**

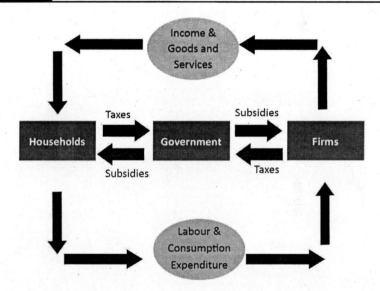

10.1.3 The four-sector economy

The financial sector is the fourth sector in the circular flow of income model. The financial sector includes not only banks but non-banking financial institutions. The role of the financial sector is to transfer money from one entity to the other. Financial institutions play an important intermediation role between households, firms, and the government. Households do not consume all that they earn. They save some of their income with banks. Furthermore, firms also deposit some of their retained profits in banks with an expectation of a higher return with interest in the future. What do banks do with this money? They lend this money to firms and governments for business and government programs respectively. Banks generate income through the difference in lending and deposit rates. Therefore, the role of financial institutions in the four-sector model is to provide firms and governments with money.

Figure 10.3 **The four-sector economy**

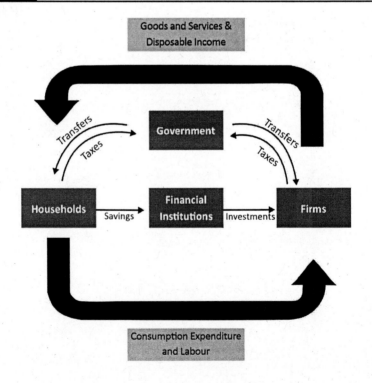

10.1.4 The five-sector economy

The fifth sector in the circular flow of income model is the foreign sector. The foreign sector interacts with the economy through the trade channel. The trade channel has two components: the export and the import of goods and services. Exports are goods and services that are produced within the domestic economy and sold to other countries in the globe. On the other hand, imports are goods and services that are produced in other countries across the globe, but consumed within the domestic economy.

The Balance of Payments is a document prepared by each country that consists of two accounts, namely, the current account and the capital account. The current account is the account that provides a description of the exports and imports of goods and services. The capital account consists of the flow of capital from the domestic country to other countries, as well the flow of capital from other countries to the domestic economy.

How does the foreign sector integrate with the circular flow of income? When a product or service is exported, there is an inflow of income to the firms and government of the domestic economy in the form of payments for the exports (known as export receipts). On the other hand, when any product or services are imported from foreign economies, there is an outflow of income when the firms and governments make payments abroad for the imports (Figure 10.4). The import payments and export receipts transactions are undertaken in the financial market. Similarly, for the capital account, when foreign economies deposit their money in the domestic economy, there is an inflow of money. When domestic residents park their income in a foreign country, there is an outflow of money. With the inclusion of the external sector, the economy now becomes an "open-economy" model.

Figure 10.4   **The five-sector economy he four-sector economy**

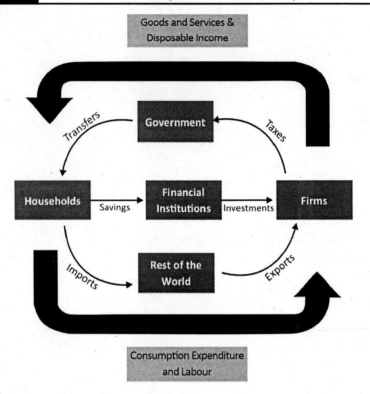

10.2 Injection and Leakages

Injections and leakages are important to understand in the context of the circular flow of income. Injections and leakages alter the income levels in an economy. An injection is defined as any activity that leads to an inflow of income to the circular flow. On the contrary, a leakage is defined as any activity that leads to a decrease in the volume of income to the circular flow. What are the variables that impact the injection and leakages in an economy?

10.2.1 Injections

Injections are any form of activities in an economy that lead to an increase in the national income of the economy. The three main constituents of injections are:

a. **Investments (I):** Investments made by firms are an important constituent of injections. Investments by firms lead to income generation through employment and contribute to an overall increase in income.

b. **Government expenditure(G):** The expenditure by the government is one of the largest contributors towards the total injections in an economy. Government expenditures are in the form of infrastructure development (roads, railways, ports, etc.), subsidies towards firms and households, and social welfare programs. These expenditures increase the overall income of an economy.

c. **Exports (X):** Exports provide revenue to the domestic economy. When goods and services are exported, export revenue is generated for the economy. Therefore, an increase in exports increases the overall income of the economy.

10.2.2 Leakages

Leakages are any form of activities in an economy that lead to a decrease in the national flow of income in the circular flow model. The three different constituents of leakages are:

a. **Savings (S):** Savings are the proportion of income by households that are not consumed and are deposited in banks and financial institutions. It flows to the financial institutions instead of the goods and services market.

Hence, it reduces the income in an economy and is considered a leakage.

b. **Taxes (T):** Taxes form a part of the revenue for the government. Taxes are paid by both households and corporations. However, taxes are considered as leakages as they flow away from the goods and services market.

c. **Imports (M):** Imports are the goods and services we buy from foreign economies. It is considered a leakage as the money paid for the import is flowing outside the economy, thereby leading to a lowering of national income.

The overall effect of national income is dependent on the balance between injections and leakages. The following conditions mentioned below demonstrate when income is at equilibrium, versus when income increases or declines.

Equilibrium income: $I + G + X = S + T + M$

Income rises when: $I + G + X > S + T + M$

Income declines when: $I + G + X < S + T + M$

When the sum of the injections is equal to the sum of the leakages, then the total flow of income is in equilibrium. If the sum of injections is greater than the leakages, the value of income increases. Conversely, if the sum of injections is lower than the leakages, the value of income declines. Therefore, whenever there is a change in the overall income of the economy, one of the six variables, or a combination of them causes the change to move either in an upward or downward direction. Table 10.1 illustrates the injections and leakages across various sectors of the economy.

Table 10.1	Injections and Leakages across various sectors	
Sector	**Income declines when**	**Income increases when**
Government Sector	*Taxes > Expenditure*	*Taxes < Expenditure*
Financial Sector	*Savings > Investment*	*Savings < Investments*
Foreign Sector	*Imports > Exports*	*Imports < Exports*

10.3 National Income

The national income is composed of the value of the goods and services that are produced within the boundaries of the economy. It is also called the Gross Domestic Product (GDP). The word final is critical, as the GDP does not take into account intermediary goods and services that are produced. Income and output are used interchangeably in macroeconomics. Hence, when the word income or output is used in this book, it is treated as one and the same. There are three different approaches to calculating the national income of an economy.

10.3.1 Production approach

The production approach is also termed as the value-added method or the Gross Value Added (GVA) method. The gross value added is defined as the output generated by each industry minus the goods and services that were used up in the process of generating that output (intermediate inputs). The final outcome is called the gross value added. For example, a baker will buy wheat, add yeast, and finally turn it into bread which will sell for more than the cost of the ingredients. The baker will also have overheads for the bakery like heating, light, and insurance. The difference between the value of the bread and the cost incurred is termed the Gross Value Added. Simply put, GVA is the value of the goods/service after eliminating all the costs involved in producing the same.

10.3.2 Income approach

The income approach uses the income generated by different factors of production in the circular flow to compute the national income. In other words, it adds up the profits generated by companies, rent earned from the capital, the wages earned by the salaried employees, and the taxes earned by the government. Thus, summing up the income earned from the different factors of production provides an estimate of the national income of the economy.

10.3.3 Expenditure approach

According to the expenditure approach, the national income of the economy is the sum total of four indicators, namely: consumption (C), Investment (I), Government expenditure (G), and Net exports (NX). The national income is then defined as:

$$Y = C + I + G + NX$$

a. **Consumption (C):** Consumption expenditure refers to the expenditure on goods and services consumed in the economy. In developed countries like the United States, consumption makes up for around 68% of the total economy[21], while in developing economies like India, consumption accounts for 60 % of the total economy. [22]

b. Investment (I): Investment, referred to as private investment is the change in the inventory stock made by firms in their business operations. It is crucial to note here that investments referred to over here are physical investments and not financial investments that households make in the capital markets. This component of investments mainly refers to (a) expenditures by businesses and firms on new factories, and machinery; (b) expenditures on real estate; and (c) changes in business inventory. Thus, if Nike adds new shoes to its stores, it is considered to be a private investment. If Apple opens up new stores, it is considered an investment. Compared to consumption, investment is more volatile and fluctuates based on the demand conditions in the market. Developed economies like the US have investments that amount to 20 % of GDP[23] while developing economies like India have investments amounting to 30% of total income. [24]

---

21. "US Private Consumption: % of GDP | Economic Indicators | CEIC."https:// www.ceicdata.com/en/indicator/united-states/private-consumption--of-nominal-gdp#:~:text=United%20States%20Private%20Consumption%20accounted,an%20 average%20share%20of%2063.3%20%25.

22. "India Private Consumption: % of GDP | Economic Indicators | CEIC." https:// www.ceicdata.com/en/indicator/india/private-consumption--of-nominal-gdp.

23. "US Investment: % of GDP | Economic Indicators | CEIC." https://www.ceicdata. com/en/indicator/united-states/investment--nominal-gdp#:~:text=United%20 States%20Investment%3A%20%25%20of%20GDP,-1947%20%2D%202023%20%7C%20 Quarterly&text=United%20States%20Investment%20accounted%20for,an%20 average%20ratio%20of%2022.3%20%25.

24. "India Investment: % of GDP | Economic Indicators | CEIC." https://www.ceicdata. com/en/indicator/india/investment--nominal-gdp#:~:text=India%20Investment%20 accounted%20for%2030.6,an%20average%20ratio%20of%2033.4%20%25.

c. **Government Expenditure (G):** Government Expenditure refers to the investments that the government makes towards infrastructure activities such as the building of roads, railways, postal infrastructure, and electricity. These are state infrastructures that generate returns through user fees and taxes. The government also provides transfer payments to a certain section of the population in the form of social security benefits to the unemployed, or pensions to the old-age. However, it is critical to note here that transfer payments are not accounted for in the national income statistics. While they are important and contribute a lot towards total government expenditure, the reason for not including them in the computation of national income is that transfer payments do not produce any goods or services in the economy.

d. **Net Exports (NX):** Net exports is defined as the difference between exports and imports. If the value is positive, it implies that exports are higher than imports. Conversely, if the value is negative, it implies that imports are higher than exports. If an American firm or an individual buys a good or service that is produced in a foreign economy, it is termed an import. On the contrary, if a foreign individual or corporation purchases a good or service from the United States, it is defined as an export for the United States.

It is important to note that the GDP that is computed by economies are estimates. Since an economy is very large, and it is impossible to track all transactions in an economy, sample surveys are conducted that lead us to such estimates. The GDP is an important metric as it portrays the growth of a nation over time. However, apart from the GDP, there are some related measures that are of interest too:

Gross National Product (GNP): The Gross National Product is defined as:

$$GNP = GDP + Net\ Factor\ Income\ from\ Abroad$$

Net factor Income from Abroad is defined as factor income earned by domestic residents in foreign economies minus factor income earned by foreign residents in the domestic economy.

Net Domestic Product (NDP): Net domestic product is defined as Gross Domestic Product minus the rate of depreciation of assets such as houses, machinery, vehicles, etc.

Gross Domestic Product at Factor Cost and Market Prices: We first need to understand what factor cost and market prices are. Factor costs are the costs associated with the production of goods and services at the factory level. Market prices are the cost of the goods and services sold at the retail (market) level. How are these two associated?

$$GDP\ (Factor\ Cost) = GDP\ (Market\ Prices) + Subsidies - Taxes$$

When the product reaches the market from the factory, the government imposes taxes, as well as provides some subsidies. Thus, the GDP at the market price is the GDP at the factory cost, plus taxes imposed on the goods and services minus the subsidies provided towards the production of those goods and services.

Gross Domestic Product at Constant versus Current Prices: The GDP is measured in both constant and current prices. Remember, GDP is the output of the goods and services produced in an economy. Thus, it is the product of the price times the quantity of items produced. When prices are marked in the current year, it is termed as GDP in current prices. On the other hand, when prices are marked in a particular base year, it is termed as GDP in constant prices.

$$GDP_{constant\ prices} = P_{base\ year} * Q_{current\ year}$$

$$GDP_{current\ prices} = P_{current\ year} * Q_{current\ year}$$

The differentiation between current and constant prices becomes important due to the following reasons. If GDP grows year on year, the growth can be achieved either through an increase in the quantity produced or purely because prices have risen. An increase GDP attributable to a price rise will only lead to inflation. Hence, GDP at constant prices depicts actual growth in output.

10.4 Conclusion

The computation of GDP through the different approaches provides an understanding of how the economy works. It is a building block towards understanding the constituents of income of an economy. The computation of GDP through the different approaches provides an understanding of how the economy works. The four important macroeconomic indicators, namely. Consumption, investment, government expenditure, and net exports are crucial in understanding the growth of the economy. Finally, assessing the different variations of the GDP such as Net Domestic Product, Gross National Product, and GDP at Factor Cost and Market Prices is vital.

Quiz

1. The circular flow of income consists of:

   a. Firms

   b. Households

   c. Government

   d. All of the above

2. The three-sector model consists of:

   a. Firms; households; and government

   b. Firms; households; and financial institutions

   c. Firms; financial institutions; and government

   d. Foreign sector; government; and households

3. The Gross Domestic Product is the _____ value of goods and services produced _____ an economy.

   a. Final; outside

   b. Final; within

   c. Intermediate; within

   d. Intermediate; outside

4. _____ are macroeconomic variables that _____ the national income of an economy.

   a. Injections; Increase

   b. Injections; Decrease

   c. Leakages; Increase

   d. Leakages; Decrease

5. The difference between Gross Domestic Product and Net Domestic Product is:

   a. Taxes

   b. Subsidies

   c. Depreciation

   d. None of the above

6. The national income of an economy increases when imports are _____ exports.

   a. Lower that

   b. Equal to

   c. Higher than

   d. None of the above

7. **The difference between GDP and GNP is _____.**

   a. Net factor income from the domestic economy

   b. Net factor income from abroad

   c. Gross factor income from the domestic economy

   d. Gross factor income from abroad

8. **The difference between GDP at market prices and GDP at factor costs is:**

   a. Subsidies and taxes

   b. Inflation

   c. Cost of transportation

   d. None of the above

9. **The difference between the output and intermediate inputs is termed as:**

   a. Gross Value Initiated

   b. Gross Value Adopted

   c. Gross Value Added

   d. None of the above

10. GDP at constant prices is the GDP adjusted for inflation:

    a. True

    b. False

    c. None of the above

    d. Cannot be determined

Answers	1 – d	2 – a	3 – b	4 – a & d	5 – c
	6 – a	7 – b	8 – a	9 – c	10 – a

Chapter Summary

◆ The circular flow of income illustrates the functioning of the economy.

◆ The simple model starts with a two-sector model and extends to the five-sector model.

◆ Injections are variables that lead to an increase in the national income of an economy. The three important injections are: Investments, exports, and government expenditure.

◆ Leakages are variables that lead to a decline in the national income of an economy. The three important leakages are: imports, taxes, and savings.

◆ The Gross Domestic Product is the sum of the final goods and services produced within the boundaries of an economy.

◆ The GDP is measured through three different approaches (a) Product Approach (b) Income Approach (c) Expenditure Approach.

◆ The product approach is also called the value-added approach which computes the GDP as the value added by each industry.

◆ The income approach computes the GDP as the sum of income generated by different factors of production.

◆ The expenditure approach computes the GDP as the sum of consumption expenditure, investment, government expenditure, and net exports.

◆ GDP at constant prices considers prices at the base year, while GDP at current prices considers prices at the current year.

◆ Gross National Product is defined as Gross Domestic Product plus Net Factor Income from Abroad.

Chapter **11**

Aggregate Demand: The Building Blocks of an Economy

This chapter discusses the factors that constitute the aggregate demand of the economy. It analyzes the consumption function and discusses the role of aggregate demand in stimulating economic growth. The chapter focuses on the role of government expenditure and explains the role of the government multiplier in an economy.

Key learning objectives of this chapter include the reader's understanding of the following:

- The role of aggregate demand in the economy
- Analyzing the importance of the consumption function in boosting economic growth

- Assessing the contribution of the marginal propensity to consume in driving consumption expenditure and economic growth

- Evaluating the government expenditure multiplier in the economy

11.1 Introduction

The price and output of an economy is determined by the aggregate demand and the aggregate supply. In the first part of this book, we discussed the concept of individual and consumer demand and the supply curve of the firm. Both the demand and supply curves were responsible for price and output generation (recall Chapter 4). In macroeconomics, the overall price and output of the economy are a function of the aggregate demand and supply curves. However, the aggregate demand and supply curves are not simply a sum of the individual demand and supply curves. Look at Figure 11.1. It illustrates the downward-sloping aggregate demand curve and the upward-sloping aggregate supply curve of the economy. The intersection point is the point of equilibrium, where the economy has reached an equilibrium price and output. Remember, GDP is simply the product of price multiplied by the quantity of the goods and services produced in the economy. The GDP of the economy is the value of the final goods and services produced and consumed in the economy. When this price level rises, it is termed inflation, while a decline in price levels leads to deflation. Similarly, when the output expands, we say that the economy is growing, and when the output is declining, we say that the economy is undergoing a recession.

But what builds up these demand and supply curves? In this chapter, we are going to focus on the building blocks of the aggregate demand curve.

Figure 11.1 **The macroeconomic equilibrium**

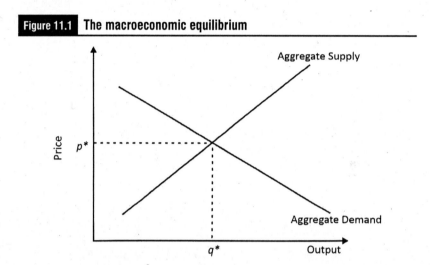

11.2 The Keynesian Economy and the Role of the Aggregate Demand

During 1929-1930, the United States faced a massive economic crisis called The Great Depression. This was the worst economic downturn that any country had ever seen. Slowing consumer demand, mounting consumer debt, and decreased industrial production were clear symptoms of the crisis. John Maynard Keynes, a famous economist of the time, emphasized the importance of aggregate demand in improving the economic condition of an economy. Keynes proposed that the only way to stimulate demand in the economy was through government spending. In other words, Keynes suggested that if the government spends money through welfare programs for individuals, and subsidies for firms, it will lead to an overall increase in consumption of the economy which will lead to higher economic growth. The aggregate demand is the sum total of four components: consumption, investment, government expenditure, and net exports. During a recessionary phase due to uncertainty looming, consumer spending is often eroded. This leads to dampened investments by firms as businesses do not see any incentive to produce. This is when Keynes proposes that state (government) intervention is necessary to stimulate the demand in an economy, which will lead to increased consumption by households and increased investments by firms. This school of thought was termed "Keynesian Economics". This belief was different from the classical school which was a proponent of the free market. A free-market proposition states that the market finds its way to reach equilibrium by itself and should not be interfered with. Keynes, however, suggested that the free market approach does not have any mechanism by which it can reach equilibrium during periods of distress and hence needs a strong government intervention.

While the four components of aggregate demand were discussed in Chapter 10, we are now going to focus a bit more on the consumption function. The consumption function plays a crucial role in the overall aggregate demand of the economy.

Consumption Function: The consumption function is a function that denotes the relationship between income and total consumption. It is denoted by the equation:

$$C = C_0 + c'Y_d$$

C_0: This is the minimum level of consumption which is not a function of income. Think of this as the basic sustenance consumption level for survival. This consumption level is financed either through borrowing or past savings.

c': This is the marginal propensity to consume. This is a very important concept in macroeconomics. The marginal propensity to consume (MPC) implies the change in consumption for a unit change in income increases. Thus, the higher the value of MPC, the higher the consumption level of the economy. The MPC is a very critical economic variable that has immense economic implications for economic growth.

Y_d: This is termed disposable income, which implies income after taxes and deductions. However, for the sake of simplicity, we will define this term as just income.

Recall the output equation from Chapter 10. It states that the output of an economy consists of consumption, investment, government expenditure, and net exports. Figure 11.2 illustrates the economic equilibrium output of an economy. Output is plotted on the horizontal axis, while aggregate demand is plotted on the vertical axis. The 45-degree line denotes that output is equal to aggregate demand. What does this imply? If you recall, the circular flow of income states that the output produced by firms is consumed by households. That loop completes the circular flow. In Figure 11.2, the 45-degree line states that all the output generated by firms is a function of the demand that is generated in an economy, such that output is equal to aggregate demand $(Y) = (AD)$. The consumption line is drawn on the same figure, with the intercept starting from the intercept starting from C_O. This denotes the 'subsistence level' of consumption. The slope of the consumption line is the level of the marginal propensity to consume (MPC). Thus, the higher the level of the MPC, the steeper will be the slope of the consumption line. This implies that as the marginal propensity to consume is higher, any increase in a component of aggregate demand will lead to a higher increase in output. In this model, we assume that government expenditure, investment, and net exports are all autonomous. By autonomous, we mean that they do not vary with changes in the income level. Point E, which is defined as the point of equilibrium, is also known as the "Keynesian Cross". This point is defined as the equilibrium where aggregate demand matches output. Any point to the right of this lies a region where output is greater than aggregate demand. This implies that more output is being produced than what is being demanded. This leads to an increased inventory of goods. A simpler way to think about this is that any point to the right of E is a point where the supply of goods is higher than the demand for goods. On the other hand, any point to the left of E is when the demand for goods is higher than the supply.

Figure 11.2 **The aggregate demand framework**

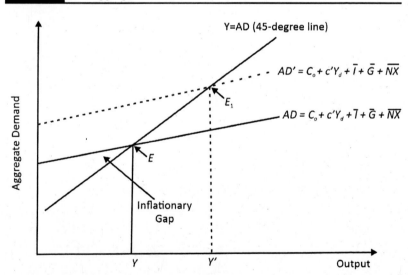

What happens if investments, government expenditure, or net exports increase? The aggregate demand line will shift upwards in a parallel manner. You will notice that when the aggregate demand line shifts upwards, the equilibrium moves to the right, leading to a higher level of output. Output increases from Y to Y_1. Similarly, if any component of aggregate demand falls, the line will shift downwards in a parallel manner. When the aggregate demand line shifts downwards, the equilibrium shifts to the left, leading to a lower level of equilibrium. Thus, when any component of aggregate demand increases, economic output increases. When aggregate demand is higher than output, the gap between the two is termed an inflationary gap. The role of central banks around the world is to reduce this inflationary gap. What is the value of economic output that is achieved in equilibrium? To understand this, look at equation 11.1

$$Y = C_o + c'Y_d + \overline{I} + \overline{G} + \overline{NX} \qquad (11.1)$$

$$Y(1 - c') = C_o + \overline{I} + \overline{G} + \overline{NX}$$

$$Y = \frac{C_0 + \overline{I} + \overline{G} + \overline{NX}}{1 - c'}$$

The equilibrium income expression states that the equilibrium level of income is a function of autonomous consumption, investment, government expenditure, and net exports. The bar sign on top of each term denotes that these are autonomous in nature (i.e., they do not change with income). This assumption is kept for simplicity at the moment. Of course, each of these factors does change and is dependent on certain macroeconomic variables. The key point here is that the equilibrium level of output is directly related to the marginal propensity to consume. As the value c' increases, $1 - c'$ falls, and therefore the entire expression increases. Thus, for every increase in the marginal propensity to consume, equilibrium income increases in the economy, and the economy grows. Today, countries that have a high level of marginal propensity to consume grow faster than other economies that have a lower marginal propensity to consume. It is important to note that even within an economy, the marginal propensity to consume changes across income levels. Low-income households would have a relatively lower MPC as compared to richer households in the same economy.

11.2.1 Autonomous expenditure multiplier

Imagine if you were given$100, and that resulted in a $10,000 dollar increase in your overall income. The jump from$100 to $10,000 is termed as the multiplier, as your income has been multiplied by 100 times. In the same way, the autonomous expenditure multiplier states that any change in any component of the autonomous expenditure will lead to a higher and multiplied effect on overall income. By how much? The quantum of the multiplier is dependent on the value of the marginal propensity to consume. Let us relook at equation 11.1. We know that $Y = \frac{C_0 + \overline{I} + \overline{G} + \overline{NX}}{1 - c'}$. The terms $C_o + \overline{I} + \overline{G} + \overline{NX}$ are termed autonomous expenditure. Let us rename them as A. Hence, equation 11.1 can be re-written as:

$$Y = \frac{A}{1 - c'}$$

Therefore, any change in A will now cause a change in Y. This can be represented as

$$\frac{\Delta Y}{\Delta A} = \frac{1}{(1 - c')} \qquad (11.2)$$

Equation 11.2 represents the autonomous expenditure multiplier. This states that when any component of autonomous expenditure changes by one unit, overall income will change by $\frac{1}{(1-c')}$. This term is called the multiplier. As you will notice, whenever c' increases, the expression increases. Hence, the autonomous expenditure multiplier is directly proportional to the value of MPC.

Keynes understood the power of the MPC and therefore emphasized that the only way to take the economy out of recession was to increase consumption. However, people can only consume when they have money. Hence, Keynes was a proponent of the role of the government in improving government expenditure, such that government expenditure will lead to higher income for households, leading to higher consumption by households and therefore higher national income.

11.3 Conclusion

The importance of government expenditure in boosting income and growth in the economy has been recognized across economies today. However, it is important that this is assessed in a cautious manner. Wasteful spending by governments in non-revenue generating expenditures can lead to high unsustainable debt. There have been countries that have spent excessively on welfare programs and subsidies that have financed government expenditure mostly through external borrowing, resulting in a situation of debt. This has caused a further downturn in the economy. The Venezuelan crisis is an example of how the economy has gone into a downturn due to wasteful spending.

Similarly, high consumer expenditure without appropriate increase in output by firms can also lead to high inflation leading to inequality of goods and services across households in the economy. Therefore, it is very important that governments are careful regarding how they allocate the budget across different sectors.

Quiz

1. The subsistence level of consumption is that proportion of consumption which is _____ to income.

   a. Independent

   b. Directly proportional

   c. Inversely related

   d. None of the above

2. The marginal propensity to consume is the same for all households within an economy.

   a. True

   b. False

   c. Cannot be determined

3. The disposable income of a household is the income net of _____.

   a. Inflation

   b. Taxes

   c. Subsidies

   d. All of the above

4. The _____ of the aggregate demand line is dependent on the _____.

    a. Intercept; marginal propensity to consume

    b. Slope; marginal propensity to save

    c. Slope; marginal propensity to consume

    d. Intercept; marginal propensity to save

5. The autonomous expenditure multiplier is _____ proportional to the _____.

    a. Directly, autonomous expenditure

    b. Inversely, marginal propensity to consume

    c. Directly, marginal propensity to consume

    d. Inversely, autonomous expenditure

6. Inflationary Gap is defined as the gap when _____ exceeds _____.

    a. Output, aggregate demand

    b. Aggregate demand, output

    c. Aggregate supply, output

    d. Output, aggregate supply

7. **Disposable income is the income that remains after _____.**

   a. Taxes

   b. Subsidies

   c. Transfers

   d. All of the above

8. **Output is a function of consumption, investment, government expenditure, and net exports.**

   a. True

   b. False

   c. Cannot be determined

9. **Net export is the difference between _____ and _____.**

   a. Exports; imports

   b. Taxes; subsidies

   c. Income; expenditure

   d. None of the above

10. If the marginal propensity to consume is high, the marginal propensity to save is _____.

    a. High

    b. Low

    c. Zero

    d. One

Answers	1 – a	2 – b	3 – b	4 – c	5 – a, c
	6 – b	7 – d	8 – a	9 – a	10 – b

Chapter Summary

◆ The four components of aggregate demand are consumption, investment, government expenditure, and net exports.

◆ Keynesian economics focuses on the role of government expenditure in stimulating demand in the economy.

◆ The marginal propensity to consume is the change in the level of consumption for any change in the level of income.

◆ The higher the marginal propensity to consume, the larger the increase in economic growth.

◆ The autonomous expenditure multiplier denotes the change in income due to a change in any component of the autonomous expenditure. The multiplier is a function of the marginal propensity to consume.

This page is intentionally left blank

Chapter **12**

Fiscal and Monetary Policy: The Toolkit for the Economy

A policy is an instrument that is used as an intervention to stimulate growth in an economy. The two important institutions whose policies affect the economy at large are the government and the central bank. Economic policy-making is difficult. The success of a policy can never be measured by one outcome, and oftentimes, certain policies could have unintended consequences. This chapter will focus on two important policies, namely, the fiscal and monetary policy. It discusses how economic policy is linked to the aggregate demand in the economy and what happens to income and prices when there are changes in policies

Key learning objectives of this chapter include the reader's understanding of the following:

- The two different types of economic policies in an economy

- Analyzing the relationship between economic policy and output and income in the economy
- Applying the functioning of the fiscal and monetary policy under different economic scenarios
- Assessing the importance of the role of the government and the central bank and how a good optimal policy mix can be achieved

12.1 Fiscal Policy

Fiscal policy is termed as the policy that is undertaken by the government of an economy. Fiscal policies could be of various types, such as welfare funds, pandemic relief funds, agricultural and manufacturing subsidies, and pensions. Different policies of the government affect different stakeholders of the economy. Recall the economic growth identity, where total income was the sum of consumption, investment, government expenditure, and net exports. The government expenditure portion of this equation primarily denotes the fiscal expenditure of the government. Governments across the globe incur expenditures on various sectors of the economy like health, education, -agriculture, etc. Furthermore, the proportion of government expenditure to overall GDP drastically varies across economies. In 2021, government expenditure constituted 30% of GDP in India, while it was 42% for the United States. In countries like Germany and France, the amount is close to 50%. [25] The amount of spending is not the only

---

25. "Correction to: Book of Abstracts ESMRMB 2023 Online 39th Annual Scientific Meeting 4–7 October 2023."*Magnetic Resonance Materials in Physics, Biology and Medicine* 37, no. 1 (December 12, 2023): 149–50. https://doi.org/10.1007/s10334-023-01130-x

important metric. The sector in which this spending is incurred plays an important role too. For example, incurring expenditure in revenue-generating activities such as investments in education, and infrastructure might be more beneficial from a budgetary standpoint than expenditures incurred purely on welfare programs.

How does government expenditure affect economic growth? The pathway by which government expenditure leads to economic growth is termed the government expenditure multiplier. Let us understand this mechanism through an example. Assume that the government spends $100,000 on building a public hospital. The public hospital can only function when there are doctors, nurses, and other support staff. Furthermore, to build the hospital, the government would need to assign contracts to construction companies. As you would notice, the decision to incur $100,000 on building a hospital generates employment for individuals. This employment is of various forms, including labor that helps in building the hospital, doctors and nurses that will run the hospital, and hospital staff that will monitor its operations. Notice that this has created an income opportunity for various households and individuals in an economy. Thus, a change in government expenditure leads to a change in the income of households and individuals. In the next stage, the households and individuals utilize this extra income to consume goods and services. Thus, consumption expenditure increases in the economy. Firms provide more goods and services to match the higher demand. To meet this demand further, firms employ more labor to work in factories to produce the extra goods and services which again increases employment and income of households and individuals and thereby increases the consumption expenditure. In Chapter 11, we established that when the consumption of households increases, the overall income of the economy increases through the multiplier effect. Figure 12.1 illustrates the mechanism by which a government expenditure can boost the national income of the economy.

Figure 12.1 **Mechanism of a multiplier effect of a government expenditure program**

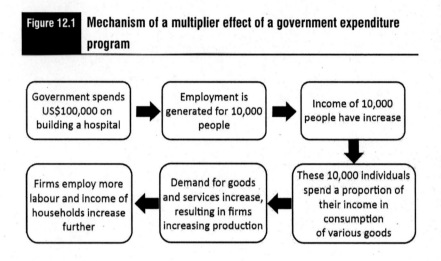

12.1.1 The government expenditure multiplier

Government expenditure is a part of the total autonomous expenditure. Recall the income equation as shown in Equation 12.1.

$$Y = C_0 + c' Y + I + NX + G$$

You will notice that now the government expenditure portion of this equation does not have a bar above it. It implies that government expenditure is changing and is not autonomous any longer. We are interested to understand the effect of a change in government expenditure on overall income:

$$Y - c'Y = C_0 + I + NX + G$$

$$Y(1 - c') = A + G$$

$$\frac{\Delta Y}{\Delta G} = \frac{1}{(1-c')}\overline{A}$$

Equation 12.2 is defined as the government expenditure multiplier. As you will notice, this is heavily dependent on the value of the MPC. The higher the MPC, the larger the value of the multiplier. Hence, when government policies are evaluated on the basis of their effectiveness, the linkage between the policy and the ability to affect MPC is examined.

12.2 Fiscal Policy and the Aggregate Demand Curve

The final macroeconomic equilibrium is at the point where aggregate demand is equal to aggregate supply. How do changes in the fiscal policy affect this equilibrium? The route by which fiscal policy affects equilibrium income is through aggregate demand. There are two kinds of fiscal policy measures. One is fiscal expansion and the second is fiscal contraction.

- **Expansionary Fiscal Policy:** A policy that is intended to increase the income of the economy is termed an expansionary fiscal policy. Governments investing in unemployment benefits, lowering taxes, and spending on healthcare and education are prime examples of expansionary fiscal policies. All of these policies have an income-enhancing effect on the economy. Any fiscal expansionary policy leads to a rightward shift of the aggregate demand curve, thereby increasing both price and output to AD_1 (Figure 12.2).

- **Contractionary Fiscal Policy:** Any fiscal policy that reduces the income of the economy is termed to be a contractionary policy. Examples of contractionary fiscal policies are: reducing welfare funds for certain sections of the society, removing subsidies to firms across various sectors, and increasing taxes for households and enterprises. All of these policies have an income-reducing effect on the economy. Look at Figure 12.2. The dotted lines represent the changes in the aggregate demand curve whenever there is contractionary fiscal policy. The aggregate demand curve shifts to the left (AD_2), leading to a decline in price and income.

Figure 12.2   **Expansionary and contractionary fiscal policies**

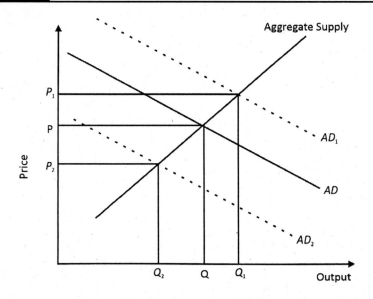

12.3 Monetary Policy and the Role of the Central Bank

Central banks across the globe have one uniform policy, which is to reduce inflation and maintain price stability. Inflation is defined as the increase in the general price levels of goods and services in the economy. How do central banks achieve this, and what effect do these policies have on overall income? Before we talk about that, let us understand why monetary policy is important. Money is important to purchase goods and services. Money has two components, namely, money demand and money supply. Money demand represents the money that is demanded by households and individuals to purchase goods and services. Money demand is a function of the interest rate provided by banks and other financial savings instruments. Imagine if you had $10,000. You decide to keep a certain proportion with you and invest the remaining in either bank deposits, mutual funds, or government securities. However, this allocation is dependent on the interest rate that is provided to you. If the interest rate offered by financial savings instruments is high, then it would pay to keep the money in those financial savings instruments and hold less cash. Thus, money demand is inversely related to interest rates in the economy. When interest rates are high, money demanded is low. When interest rates are low, money demanded is high. Inflation is a scenario when more money is chasing fewer goods. When the output of goods and services is limited, but the money that individuals have is in excess, then households and individuals are willing to spend more for the same good and service. This causes an increase in price, causing inflation.

Central banks regulate the interest rate on observing the level of inflation in the economy. High inflation rates leads central banks to increase the interest rate, thereby encouraging households to invest in financial savings instruments. On the other hand, when inflation is very low (i.e., households are not purchasing goods and services), the central banks lower the interest rates to ensure that the money demand is high in the economy and households spend money on purchasing goods and services. All economic crises in the past have been followed by periods of low-interest rates. Right from the Great Depression in the 1930s to the Asian economic crisis in the late 1990s and the pandemic in 2020, central banks have responded to each of these crises by reducing interest rates so as to stimulate spending in the economy.

12.3.1 Monetary policy and the aggregate demand

Just like fiscal policies, monetary policy is linked to changes in aggregate demand. Monetary policy is of two types:

- **Expansionary Monetary Policy:** In an expansionary monetary policy, the central bank reduces the interest rate so as to stimulate spending and consumption in the economy which will lead to high economic growth and higher income. This leads to higher output levels in the economy (Figure 12.2).

- **Contractionary Monetary Policy:** A contractionary monetary policy is aimed to reduce prices and output in the economy. Increasing interest rates would incentivize households to save their money in financial savings instruments, and thereby reduce their consumption expenditure. A contractionary monetary policy leads to a leftward shift of the aggregate demand curve leading to a decrease in price and income in the economy (similar to the expansionary fiscal policy). The effect is illustrated in Figure 12.2.

12.4 Policy Mix and Lag Effect

The interplay of both fiscal and monetary policies is important. It is important to understand that both these policies have their own lag effects. **Lag effects** denote the time between the policy announcement and its effect on the economy. Fiscal policies and monetary policies have different lag effects. At times, when the lag effect is too long, it makes the policy redundant. Consider this example. In 1960, during the era of President John F. Kennedy, there was a proposal to reduce taxes to combat recession. The President recommended it to Congress in 1962, and it was not passed until 1964, three years after the recession had ended. It was felt that the long implementation lag made this tool ineffective. This is one example of how a long lag effect can have undesirable consequences. It is difficult to say which policy (between fiscal and monetary) has a shorter lag because it largely depends on the economy at that point in time as well as the specific policy that is being proposed. However, it is important to note that policymakers and households should recognize these lag effects and act accordingly.

We have spoken about fiscal and monetary policy in isolation. However, in reality, there is some sort of a policy mix. A policy mix is when the fiscal and monetary policy is implemented together. It is recommended that the government (the actor deciding on the fiscal policy), and the central bank (the actor deciding on the monetary policy) should be in alignment as that would help reach the final objective faster. However, if one policy counteracts the other, the intended objective may not always be reached. Consider an example where the economy is in a downturn and the government wishes to increase the income of the economy. It pursues an expansionary fiscal policy through a mix of policy instruments such as lowering taxes and providing subsidies. This shifts the aggregate demand curve to the right. On the contrary, if the central bank raises interest rates, it will incentivize people to save more and spend less. Therefore, the monetary policy and the fiscal policy would result in crossroads with each other.

12.5 The Aggregate Supply Curve

Supply-side economics play an important role in the economic growth process. Supply shocks are either positive or negative. A positive supply shock is raises output in the economy. These could be lowered prices of inputs, lower wage rates for labor, higher availability of raw materials, etc. All these factors positively affect supply and move the supply curve to the right. On the other hand, factors that lead to a reduced supply will cause price and income to reduce. These are factors such as the high price of inputs, higher wage rates for labor, and lower availability of raw materials. All of these factors cause a supply shock, leading to the supply curve shifting to the left and resulting in a fall in income and price. Figure 12.4 illustrates the shifts in the aggregate supply curve and the effects on price and income. Any supply side-effects can be counteracted by demand-side policies that have been described before.

12.6 Conclusion

Economic policy-making is difficult. It is an art to be able to craft and execute a policy to reach an intended objective in mind. Policies affect various stakeholders at different levels. It affects individuals and households, and it affects firms as well as foreign economies. Certain policies have spillover effects across various economies and stakeholders. It is important that the central bank and the government are in alignment with the policy decisions that are being implemented in order to have a successful and smooth functioning of the economy.

Quiz

1. A fiscal policy is a policy that is controlled by _____.

    a. Central bank

    b. Government

    c. Judiciary

    d. None of the above

2. A monetary policy is a policy that is controlled by the _____.

    a. Government

    b. Central bank

    c. Judiciary

    d. Both a and b

3. An expansionary fiscal policy _____ income and _____ price levels.

    a. Decreases; increases

    b. Decreases; decreases

    c. Increases; decreases

    d. Increases; increases

4. **A contractionary fiscal policy _____ income and _____ price levels.**

   a. Decreases; decreases

   b. Increases; increases

   c. Decreases; increases

   d. Increases; decreases

5. **An expansionary monetary policy _____ income and _____ price levels.**

   a. Decreases; increases

   b. Decreases; decreases

   c. Increases; decreases

   d. Increases; increases

6. **A contractionary monetary policy _____ income and _____ price levels.**

   a. Decreases; decreases

   b. Increases; increases

   c. Decreases; increases

   d. Increases; decreases

7. **The government expenditure multiplier depends _____ on the _____.**

   a. Directly; Marginal propensity to consume

   b. Inversely; Marginal propensity to consume

   c. Directly; Marginal propensity to save

   d. None of the above

8. **Labor shortages due to a strike are termed as a _____ supply shock which will shift the supply curve to the _____.**

   a. Negative; left

   b. Positive; right

   c. Negative, right

   d. Positive, left

9. **A policy mix is a combination of a _____ policy and a _____ policy with the intention to reach the _____ objective.**

   a. Fiscal; monetary; same

   b. Fiscal; monetary; different

   c. Inflation; exchange rate; same

   d. Inflation; exchange rate; different

10. In an economy, the income of consumers has declined. The government has introduced a stimulus program in the budget to provide subsidies to a large section of the economy. This is a case of a _____ .

a. Fiscal policy

b. Monetary policy

c. Both a and b

d. None of the above

Answers	1 – b	2 – b	3 – d	4 – a	5 – d
	6 – a	7 – a	8 –a	9 – a	10 – a

Chapter Summary

◆ A policy is an instrument by either the government or the central bank with an objective to achieve a specific objective.

◆ Fiscal policy is a policy undertaken by the government, while monetary policy is a policy undertaken by the central bank.

◆ Policies can either enhance income or reduce income. Policies that increase income are termed expansionary policies, while policies that reduce income are contractionary policies.

◆ An expansionary policy shifts the aggregate demand curve outwards to the right and increases price and output.

◆ A contractionary policy shifts the aggregate demand curve below to the left and reduces price and output.

◆ The government expenditure multiplier examines how income changes (multiplies) when there is a change in the government expenditure.

◆ The government expenditure multiplier is proportional to the marginal propensity to consume.

◆ Fiscal and monetary policies have different lag effects.

◆ Supply shocks cause movements in the aggregate supply curve. Positive supply shocks shift the supply curve to the right, while negative supply shocks shift the supply curve to the left.

Glossary

This glossary defines key terms used throughout the book, offering readers clarity on important concepts and jargon in the field of economics.

Absolute Advantage – The ability to produce a good using fewer inputs than another producer

Average product – The total output of the firm divided by the total amount of the respective input used

Comparative Advantage – The ability to produce a good at a lower opportunity cost than another producer

Constant returns to scale – A proportional change in the output to the change in the input

Consumer Surplus – The surplus generated due to the difference in the market price and the willingness to pay by the consumer

Cross-price elasticity – The percentage change in quantity demanded for one good caused due to the percentage change in price of the other related good

Decreasing returns to scale – A less-than-proportional change in the output to a proportional change in the input

Economies of Scale – The cost advantage a firm achieves due to a higher scale of production

Economies of Scope – The cost advantage of producing two goods together, rather than producing them separately

First-mover advantage – The advantage received by starting first in a game

Fiscal Policy – The use of taxes and expenditure by the government to boost the economy

Fixed Cost – The cost incurred by the firm irrespective of the level of output

Fiscal policy – The use of taxes and expenditures by the government to grow the economy

Fixed cost – The cost incurred by the firm irrespective of the level of output

Increasing returns to scale – A higher than proportional change in the output to a proportional change in the input

Inflation – The rate of change in overall prices in an economy

Indifference Curves – Graphical representation of consumer preferences that illustrates the different choices of a consumer at the same utility level

Law of diminishing marginal returns – The marginal returns to consumption or production that decrease as the same input is consumed over time

Marginal propensity to consume – The marginal change in consumption due to a change in disposable income

Marginal rate of substitution – The rate of substitution of one good for another, keeping the utility level of the consumer constant

Monetary policy – The use of tools such as interest rates by the central bank to keep a check on inflation in the economy

Marginal cost – The change in variable cost due to a marginal change in the input

Marginal product – The change in total output, due to a marginal change in input

Marginal revenue – The change in total revenue due to a marginal change in output sold

Monopoly – A market condition where there is only one seller in the market

Nash Equilibrium – An equilibrium wherein the strategy of each of the players is the best response given the other person's strategy such that there is no participant can gain by changing his/her own strategy

Net exports – The difference between exports and imports in an economy

Oligopoly – A market condition where there are few sellers concentrated in the market

Price discrimination – The practice of charging different prices to different sets of consumers.

Price elasticity – The percentage change in quantity (demanded or supplied) by the percentage change in price

Producer surplus – The surplus generated due to the difference in the market price and the cost of production for the producer

Returns to scale – The change in output due to a change in input

Social welfare – The sum of consumer surplus and producer surplus in an economy

Simultaneous games – A game where both players make their moves simultaneously

Sequential games – A game where one player starts first, and the other players respond later

Utility – The satisfaction achieved on consuming a particular good

Variable Cost – The cost incurred due to the use of variable inputs in production

Bibliography

1. Belleflamme, Paul & Peitz, Martin, 2021. "The Economics of Platforms: Concepts and Strategy,"

2. Dean, E., Elardo, J., Green, M., Wilson, B., & Berger, S. (2016). Principles of Microeconomics: Scarcity and Social Provisioning\. Open Oregon Educational Resources.

3. Eliana Eitches and Vera Crain, "Using gasoline data to explain inelasticity," Beyond the Numbers: Prices and Spending, vol. 5, no. 5 (U.S. Bureau of Labor Statistics, March 2016), https://www.bls.gov/opub/btn/volume-5/using-gasoline-data-to-explain-inelasticity.htm

4. Frey, B. S. (1999). Economics as a science of human behavior: Towards a new social science paradigm. Springer Science & Business Media.

5. Mullainathan, S., & Shafir, E. (2013). Scarcity: Why having too little means so much. Macmillan.

6. M. E. The Competitive Advantage: Creating and Sustaining Superior Performance. NY: Free Press, 1985. (Republished with a new introduction, 1998.)

Notes